Love Revolution

REDISCOVERING THE LOST COMMAND OF JESUS

Revised Edition

GAYLORD ENNS

LOVE revolution PRESS

Cover design by Erin Mathis, www.emdesignstudio.com
Author photo by Marty Hayworth, mlhphoto@sbcglobal.net

Published by: Love Revolution Press
P.O. Box 6790
Chico, CA 95927-6790
www.LoveRevolutionPress.com
info@LoveRevolutionPress.com

DEDICATION

Most of you will never know my dad, Herman. He comes from stoic German stock. He was one of fourteen children born to an immigrant from the Ukraine, Dietrich Enns, and his wife, Sara. They had seven boys and seven girls. Dad is the oldest boy.

We just celebrated his ninety-ninth birthday. He still mows his own lawn. A few weeks ago, I helped Dad repair a broken fence post in his backyard. By the time I arrived, he had already dug the hole. That's Dad!

Vocationally, he was a dairy farmer, carpenter and building contractor. He and my (late) mother, Katie, had four children, three girls and then a boy. Mom is in heaven now. She left us just after Christmas in 1969.

When Dad married Iris in 1971, it was as if God sent us a special gift to fill a huge hole in our hearts. For thirty-seven years, Iris has been mom to us. She is the only grandmother our children have ever known.

It's to my dad that I dedicate this book.

Dear Dad,

It is an honor to dedicate this book to you. I've had the privilege of learning from many, but without question, I've learned more from you than any other person on the planet.

You are such an important part of this story. Some of my earliest memories are of the little country church we attended. You gathered us in the family room each evening to read from the

Bible and to kneel in prayer together before bedtime. The values you demonstrated made a lasting impression on us.

You continue to have such a significant place in our lives. We treasure your daily prayers for us—your children, grand-children, great-grandchildren and great-great-grandchildren.

We are so glad you are still here with us. Thanks, Dad, for all your hard work and for helping to make our Christian faith a daily reality.

It is with deep gratitude that I dedicate this book to you.

I love you, Dad!

Your son,

Gaylord

March 2008

WORDS OF APPRECIATION

A thousand thank-yous go out with this book. So many of you have supported Patti and me as we launched a whole new mission late in life—investing in pastors and next-generation leaders and in writing this book. Your friendship, giving and prayers have been invaluable to us.

We have been encouraged repeatedly by a circle of close friends. Some of you are in Christian ministry, others in secular vocations and still others devoted to raising a family. We owe a debt of love to each of you. Thank you so much for your help and encouragement along the way!

To our children and family, you have been an amazing source of inspiration to us. Your affirmation of this message has given us courage at pivotal stages of writing. Your constant love is priceless. You bring us so much joy in the journey. Thank you!

To Chico pastors, you have had a very significant role in my completing this book. Many of the thoughts in it were nurtured in the context of our fellowship. You listened to my early ideas and provided many meaningful comments. Although I do not assume your agreement with all that I have written here, you have affirmed the importance of Jesus' Command. Thank you!

To my small group, you have been the friends everyone dreams of having. Our weekly time together over the past thirteen years has been used by God to make this journey possible. You have helped me process life and the ideas in this book. More than words can express, thank you for being my friends.

Patti, you are the "wife of my youth," and you continue to grow more beautiful with time. You are a treasure to me. Thanks so much for believing in me and being a vibrant part of my life—nearly forty years now. Your faith and partnership with me in this season are such a gift. I would not be where I am today without your love and hard work. Thanks, Babe, for your countless hours of reading and helpful suggestions.

To my friends, thank you for reading the early manuscript and helping to refine the message. To Carol Lane, my heartfelt thanks for your many hours of editing of both the first and revised editions. Your help was such a gift to me, one I couldn't have done without.

To Mary McDonald and Larry Jerden, this revised second edition is a product of your vision and hard work. As editors, your passionate commitment to both the message in *Love Revolution* and to seeing this revised edition completed has been a treasured gift to me and to all who will read it. I owe a huge debt of gratitude to both of you.

Above all, thank You, God, for Your mercies that are new every morning. Knowing You as Father, Son and Holy Spirit is a mystery and yet a reality without which I couldn't survive. Your promises and presence have made all the difference in my life. All that I am, I offer again to You.

CONTENTS

INTRODUCTION

"The only thing constant in life is change."[1] These oft-quoted words were penned by François de la Rochefoucauld, a seventeenth-century philosopher.

In contrast, Malachi, the last of the Old Testament prophets, speaking as an oracle of God in the fifth century B.C., wrote, "I am the LORD, I change not."[2]

I agree with both. From between our life experience of constant change and the God who does not change, comes this book. It is born out of the stuff of life. It comes out of pain and brokenness, yet results in peace, joy and hope. It is rooted in the God who does not change, yet reserves the right to make profound change in us and in the world He created.

The truth that is at the core of this book will never change. It will never change because it is founded in the nature and character of God, who said, "I change not." But our understanding of that truth will change us.

Love Revolution is about loss, discovery and recovery. It is about coming full circle, back to the point of origin and the One who will never change. It is about returning to the feet of the Master Teacher—Jesus.

Welcome to the adventure!

---

[1] Copyright © ThinkExist 1999-2006, thinkexist.com
[2] Malachi 3:6 KJV

CHAPTER 1

DAYS GONE AWRY

Sunday, October 21, 2001, started like a thousand other Sunday mornings before it. We all have our routines. As a pastor, mine was to get up at 4:30 a.m.—5 at the latest—then shower, shave and dress for the Sunday services I had been preparing for all week.

I'd learned early in my pastoral ministry that it was especially important on Sunday mornings "to give no place to the devil."[1] If anything could go wrong, it would go wrong on that day. So as a pastor, I treasured time alone in those early morning hours—time to focus my heart and mind for a very demanding day. Now, with thirty-four years of full-time Christian ministry under my belt, getting up and out early was a well-established habit. It was just after 5:30 that morning when I quietly closed our front door and, with briefcase in hand, walked to my car.

Our city of under 100,000 people had very few eating places open that early. Denny's diner had been my Sunday morning quiet spot for years. Often the waitress would have seen me driving up to the near-empty restaurant and turned in my standard order. By the time I got my Bible and sermon notes positioned on the table, water and extra napkins would be waiting for me in the quiet corner booth.

---

[1] See Ephesians 4:27 KJV

But this October morning, something pulled me off course. I wasn't heading down the freeway to the off-ramp that would take me to my familiar corner booth at Denny's. Rather, I was driving aimlessly down empty streets toward downtown. Without fully realizing what I was doing, I parked at the curb in front of a small, unfamiliar donut shop.

When I stepped up to the glass display a second time and pointed to another donut, it began to dawn on me that something was very different—wrong. I wrestled momentarily with a silent question, "Do you have to pay for refills here?" With my thumbnail, I subconsciously pressed little grooves into the rim of the Styrofoam cup in my hand.

As I sat alone at that unfamiliar table, I knew something wasn't working. Something was broken. I needed help. I couldn't be with people this morning. The thought of speaking at two Sunday morning services loomed before me like impassable canyons.

I stepped out on the sidewalk, cell phone in hand, and called my twenty-seven-year-old son, one of my associate pastors. It was 5:50 a.m. I got Eric's answering machine and left a brief message asking him to call me. Then quickly I dialed the number of another pastor, remembering that he had once volunteered, "If you ever need help, call me!"

"Thank God for friends like him," I thought as the phone rang.

"Hello," a quiet, sleepy voice on the other end of the line answered. It was my friend's wife.

"Hi, this is Gaylord," I said. "I'm sorry, but I'm not doing well this morning. I need some help, and I'm calling to see if Tom could speak for me today."

"He would do anything to help you, but he's not here. He's speaking at a retreat this weekend."

Just my luck. I'd never had to take someone up on this kind of offer before, and the first time I really needed help, they weren't available. Standing in the middle of the sidewalk in the early morning air, I felt numb. What should I do next?

Mercifully my cell phone rang, interrupting my question. It was my son. "Hey, Dad, we unplugged our phone last night so I didn't get your call till just now."

"Son, I . . . I'm not doing well. I'm not making it today. Could you speak for me?"

There was a brief moment of silence. "No worries, Dad. No worries."

I'll never forget those two little words: "No worries." They were my introduction to a much deeper brokenness than I could imagine, but more than that, they were the first drops of soothing oil I needed to repair my broken emotional condition. Those two words were the beginning of a season of healing that would bring a powerful explosion of truth and change my life forever.

HOW DEEP IS THIS HOLE?

Looking back on it, this day hadn't come without warning. I had not been sleeping well for months. I was starting to stutter when I spoke. Decisions were getting harder to make. Increasingly, I had been experiencing depression and was under a doctor's care and taking the antidepressant he prescribed. But the depression was not the kind that people in my congregation could see. Like a layer of thick fog, it settled over me at the end of a long and exhausting day.

My staff and the elders of our congregation lifted all responsibilities off me and released me into a sabbatical season to facilitate my recovery. I slept for a month and a half. I don't mean that I slept twenty-four hours a day. I just generally slept—morning, afternoon and night. I was tired, drained and depleted. I didn't—couldn't—read any books. A couple of times, I started to watch a program on TV, but after a few minutes, I would lose focus. "Why would anyone ever want to watch this?"

What I could do was listen to CNN. The drone of anonymous voices in the background actually helped me do what I wanted to do most—sleep!

This was hard on my wife, Patti. I remember one day about three weeks into my breakdown. I had just finished eating the sandwich she had fixed me for lunch and was lying back down on the couch when I saw her standing over me.

"Honey, you're scaring me! You slept all night. You napped all morning. If you sleep this afternoon, aren't you afraid you won't be able to sleep tonight?"

"Babe, I can hardly wait until tonight so I can go to bed!"

After a month of this, my worry grew. I couldn't shake the thoughts: "How deep is this hole? How far will I fall? When I hit bottom, what will it look like? Will I ever have the strength to climb out? How long will this extreme fatigue last?"

Following my burnout, our church elders asked me to see a Christian counselor. The two hours I had each week with this trusted professional provided a wonderful oasis for me. It was a place to process and gain needed understanding of the issues that had contributed to my descent into this broken state.

Yet my persistent fatigue was disturbing to both Patti and me. I sought additional help and was told, "Trust your body. When your body has had the rest it needs, it will tell you." And sure enough, after six weeks of mostly sleep, natural energy started to return—very slowly. I didn't want to sleep all day *and* all night.

As Christmas approached, one of the first small tasks I tackled was putting up the outdoor lights on our home. In years past, this job had always been an unwelcome intrusion into my busy schedule. It involved finding which of the large plastic storage boxes in the garage marked "Christmas Decorations" actually had the lights in it. After clearing that hurdle, I would untangle the strands and string them around the eaves while balancing on a ladder that seemed to shift constantly in the rain-soaked flower-beds. Then came the magical moment when I'd plug them in and step back to see . . . that two of the strands remained unlit, like a big mocking grin with a couple of missing teeth. Ugh!

But this time, I had all day. I plugged in each strand before stringing them, separating them into those that worked and those that needed repair. Then I patiently and deliberately worked over the strands that were defective, examining each bulb until I found the faulty one and replaced it.

When I stepped back this year to look at the Christmas "stars" that outlined the front of our home, I had a small sense of the Creator's joy. "And God saw that it was good."

It had been a long time since I had experienced that sense of satisfaction about anything, especially Christmas lights! But by far, the best was yet to come. God was repairing the "burned-out bulbs" in my life. And when the "lights" came back on, my spiritual worldview would be changed dramatically. But first, there was one more challenge.

AN UNPLEASANT SURPRISE

For the first time, I was facing the fact that I was the steward of something more than my spiritual well-being. I had a soul that needed care and a body that I could no longer neglect, even for a cause as lofty as pastoral ministry. My annual physical examination had been scheduled well before my breakdown, and by the time it rolled around in December, I was taking a more proactive approach to my overall health.

My doctor had just finished the exam. He was sitting at a small table near me, writing some notes in my chart. I was buttoning my shirt. "Doctor, should I be getting one of those 'colon things'?"

"How old are you?" he asked, without looking up.

"Fifty-six."

"Yes," he said, scribbling a brief note on his prescription pad. "We'll set up the colonoscopy and call you with the date and time."

They scheduled the procedure for two months later. That left Patti and me free to enjoy our first Christmas ever without the extra planning and activities that pastors experience during this season. And it allowed me time to continue the healing process.

The middle of January brought a significant milestone in my recovery. As I was showering one morning, I had my first creative thought in months. It was wonderful. Minutes later, as I stood drying off, I could not, for the life of me, remember what that creative thought had been. But just knowing that I had had one was enough for that day!

Early March rolled around. My colonoscopy was uneventful except for one small polyp the doctor found and removed. The next day, Patti and I drove to Southern California for the weekend. Thoughts of the procedure were forgotten as we enjoyed time together with our daughter, Erin, and her husband near the beach in Santa Monica. I didn't give any more thought to it until the weekend was over and we were winding our way back home. We had just passed over the twisty grade of I-5 called The Grapevine when Patti reminded me that I should call to get the results of the biopsy.

I dialed the number of my doctor's office, and a woman at the front desk put me through to him. "Hi, this is Gaylord Enns. I'm calling to get the results of my test from last week."

"Where are you calling from?"

"My wife and I are driving up I-5. We just came over The Grapevine. We've been in L.A. visiting family."

"You're on a cell phone then?"

"Yes."

"Possibly it would be better if you call me when you get back to Chico."

"Actually, it's fine to talk now. There's very little traffic on I-5 today."

"Are you by yourself?"

"No. My wife is here with me in the car." I was starting to feel slightly irritated. It was as if he wasn't really listening to me.

"Would you like to pull over?"

At that moment, it dawned on me that the doctor had something to say that he wasn't sure I was ready to hear. It had never occurred to me that the colonoscopy was anything more than a routine procedure. After all, I had spontaneously requested it.

"Doctor, I live with a lot of peace. Whatever you have to tell me, you can say it now."

"The biopsy showed some cells with marked dysplasia. We will need to do some follow-up surgery. I have two surgeons I can recommend."

It was obvious to me that "marked dysplasia" were code words the doctor was using to protect me from what he was really saying.

"Doctor, does this have anything to do with cancer?"

"Why don't you call me tomorrow when you get into town?"

The next day, the doctor invited me into his office. Looking across his desk at me, he confirmed the news. It was cancer. They been able to find a margin of clear tissue around the polyp that he'd removed.

"Please don't be mad at me if we don't find more cancer," he said, "but I can't sleep without knowing if we got it all. If you were eighty-five I wouldn't worry about it, but at your age, I can't risk the possibility."

A week later, they had taken out a foot and a half of my colon along with the lymphatic system associated with that section. The good news was that they found no more cancer.

My recovery from this major surgery took the balance of March and all of April. That brought me to the month of May and a day that would revolutionize my understanding of what it means to be a follower of Jesus.

CHAPTER 2

AN EMPTY TABLE

May 1, 2002, is a day I will never forget. I awakened that Wednesday morning with a very clear thought: "I'm ready to study the Bible!"

For me there was great joy in that declaration. The excitement I felt was heightened by the fact that I hadn't studied the Bible or prepared a sermon for half a year. As a pastor with a teaching gift, studying the Scriptures had been a very life-giving part of who I was. Now I was back and excited to be awake after what felt like a long, dark night.

Settling in at our kitchen table to study God's Word that morning, I had the sense that I was sitting down at a large empty desk, one that had once been filled with many important tasks. Now that desk had been tipped over, everything filling my life had slid off and in its place only one thing remained — my Bible.

I *was* ready to study God's Word. But *where* would I start? The Bible is a big book! Should I start in Genesis? Psalms? One of the Gospels? Revelation? I needed a place, a topic or a point of focus to actually begin what I was ready to do that day.

It was in that moment that the Great Commission came to my mind. I opened my laptop computer Bible to Matthew 28:18 and read these familiar words:

All authority in heaven and on earth has been given to me. Therefore go and make disciples of all nations, baptizing them in the name of the Father and of the Son and of the Holy Spirit, and teaching them to obey everything I have commanded you. And surely I am with you always, to the very end of the age.[1]

An almost warming sense went through me as my eyes focused on the comforting words displayed on the screen. These words were literally the reason I had become a pastor. I had ministered to people on the authority of the Great Commission for thirty-four years. This passage had been the theme of some of my most passionate sermons and teachings throughout those decades of Christian ministry.

Quickly, my attention shifted to the other half of the split screen on my laptop. When I was preparing my last sermon six months earlier, I had been referencing a Bible text in Robert Young's *Literal Translation of the Bible.*

Given to me was all authority in heaven and on earth; having gone, then, disciple all the nations, (baptizing them—to the name of the Father, and of the Son, and of the Holy Spirit, teaching them to observe all, whatever I did command you) and lo, I am with you all the days—till the full end of the age.[2]

Immediately I was struck with Young's use of the parentheses. Apparently he had chosen to use the parenthetical enclosure because he thought it brought clarity to the instruction Jesus was giving. From my understanding of Young's translation, I paraphrased what Jesus was saying like this:

---

[1] Matthew 28:18-20
[2] Matthew 28:18-20 *Young's Literal Translation*

I have been given all authority in heaven and on earth. Wherever you go, *make disciples of all the nations,* and know this; I am with you every day until the very end. (By the way, if you need to be reminded of what making disciples is all about, I'm embedding a two-part definition for you: [1] baptizing them in the name of the Father, and of the Son and of the Holy Spirit, and [2] teaching them to obey all that I commanded you.)

Evidently, Young viewed the parenthetical phrase as Jesus' own embedded definition of disciple making. In other words, he believed that Jesus was not just telling them *what to do*—disciple the nations—but also *how to do it.* If my brain had been wired to an excitement meter in that moment, it would have registered off the scale. Jesus had actually embedded His own definition of disciple making in the Great Commission, a definition that contained two parts—(1) *baptizing them* and (2) *teaching them.*

The first part—*baptizing them*—seemed to be tied directly to faith in Jesus Christ. Believing in Him was the first step in discipleship and led to baptism, a formal declaration of one's faith in Jesus. For the new believer, baptism was a point of identification as one of Jesus' disciples.

The second part—*teaching them*—was the process of communicating to those newly initiated believers everything Jesus had commanded His original disciples to obey. Frankly, it had never seemed as clear or as simple to me as it did in that moment. Excitement reverberated in me as these simple insights dawned on a mind that had been flat-lined for months!

I had done a fair amount of evangelism over the years. I had shared the Good News with thousands and watched as many put their faith in Jesus. During decades of pastoral ministry, I had baptized hundreds of people. I felt I had a good understanding of the *baptizing them* half of discipleship.

But for some reason, the *teaching them* half captured my attention in that moment. *What all had Jesus commanded His disciples to obey?* In that moment, I knew I needed to find the answer to that question. That would be the focus of my first Bible study.

Little did I know that before that day was over, I would be shaken with a profound new realization. May 1, 2002, would mark the start of a voyage that, when complete, would change my understanding of disciple making forever.

An amazing journey had begun.

CHAPTER 3

ALL THAT I COMMANDED

My study would focus on finding the answer to the question: *What all had Jesus commanded His disciples to obey?* My goal would be to find the ten, twenty, forty or more things that Jesus had commanded. Then I planned to systematize them into a logical format, one I could use to teach new Christians.

Because Jesus had said "teaching them to obey everything I have *commanded* you,"[1] I would start my study with the obvious—the word "commanded" as found right there in the Great Commission. In the Greek language, the word "commanded" is *entellomai*. I typed this word and a closely related word, *entole*, into my computer and pressed the enter key. In an instant, the eightyseven times they were used in the New Testament flashed across the screen.

I printed out the verses that contained either of these two words and started to read. I found that fifteen times when the word "commanded" was used, it directed someone, or a small group of people, to take some immediate action. Because it was an action uniquely commanded of them at that time, there was no ongoing application for us today. For example, Jesus used this word "commanded" to prohibit Peter, James and John from prematurely

---

[1] Matthew 28:20

telling others what they had seen when He was transfigured before them on the mountain.

> As they were coming down from the mountain, Jesus *commanded (entellomai)* them, saying, "Tell the vision to no one until the Son of Man has risen from the dead."[2]

I found a second way the word "command" was used. Nearly forty times in the New Testament it was used in reference to the *commandments* found in the Law of Moses. For example, Jesus said the following in answer to a question:

> You know the *commandments (entole)*: "Do not murder, do not commit adultery, do not steal, do not give false testimony, do not defraud, honor your father and mother."[3]

However, it was the third way that the word "command" was used that surprised me and gripped my attention. I found the word "command" used in the company of the word "love" more than thirty times! The connection between these two words—"command" and "love"—startled me. I read them and then I re-read them aloud, just to let the words sink in.

> A new *command* I give you: *Love* one another. As I have *loved* you, so you must *love* one another. By this all men will know that you are my disciples, if you *love* one another.[4]

> If you *love* me, you will obey what I *command*. . . . Whoever has my *commands*[5] and obeys them, he is the one who *loves* me. He who *loves* me will be *loved* by my Father, and I too

---

[2] Matthew 17:9 NAS
[3] Mark 10:19
[4] John 13:34-35
[5] For commentary on the mixed use of plural "commands" and singular "command," see Appendix A.

will *love* him and show myself to him. . . . The world must learn that I *love* the Father and that I do exactly what my Father has *commanded* me.[6]

If you obey my *commands*, you will remain in my *love*, just as I have obeyed my Father's *commands* and remain in his *love*. . . . My *command* is this: *Love* each other as I have *loved* you. Greater *love* has no one than this, that he lay down his life for his friends. You are my friends if you do what I *command*. . . . This is my *command: Love* each other.[7]

The *commandments*, "Do not commit adultery," "Do not murder," "Do not steal," "Do not covet," and whatever other *commandment* there may be, are summed up in this one rule: "*Love* your neighbor as yourself." *Love* does no harm to its neighbor. Therefore *love* is the fulfillment of the law.[8]

[We] receive from him [God] anything we ask, because we obey his *commands* and do what pleases him. And this is his *command:* to believe in the name of his Son, Jesus Christ, and to *love* one another as he *commanded* us. Those who obey his *commands* live in him, and he in them.[9]

We *love* because he first *loved* us. If anyone says, "I *love* God," yet hates his brother, he is a liar. For anyone who does not *love* his brother, whom he has seen, cannot *love* God, whom he has not seen. And he has given us this *command:* Whoever *loves* God must also *love* his brother.[10]

This is how we know that we *love* the children of God: by *loving* God and carrying out his *commands*. This is *love* for

---

[6] John 14:15, 21, 31
[7] John 15:10, 12-14, 17
[8] Romans 13:9-10
[9] 1 John 3:22-24
[10] 1 John 4:19-21

God: to obey his *commands*. And his *commands* are not burdensome.[11]

I am not writing you a new *command* but one we have had from the beginning. I ask that we *love* one another. And this is *love:* that we walk in obedience to his *commands*. As you have heard from the beginning, his *command* is that you walk in *love*.[12]

For the first time, I saw the striking relationship between the words "command" and "love" in the New Testament. More important, I saw that this relationship had its origin in the New Command that Jesus had given His disciples on the night before His crucifixion! This connection between the words "command" and "love" was not just an important theme that Peter, James, John or Paul had introduced in their writings. Rather, loving one another, as they taught it, was rooted in nothing less than the New Command that Jesus gave to His disciples!

A *new command* I give you: *Love one another*. As I have loved you, so you must *love one another*. By this all men will know that you are my disciples, if you *love one another*.[13]

On that pivotal evening, Jesus did more than introduce it as a new command. He took ownership of it, calling it "My command," and He repeated it two more times before the night was over.

My command is this: Love each other as I have loved you.[14]

---

[11] 1 John 5:2-3
[12] 2 John 1:5-6
[13] John 13:34-35
[14] John 15:12

This is *my command:* Love each other.[15]

Immediately, I was confronted with (and it seemed like for the first time) *Jesus' Commandment.* This was more than another teaching. It had the full weight of the word "command" as used in the Ten Commandments found in the Law of Moses.

For the first time, I found myself considering the possibility that Jesus may have given us only *one command!* How could I have missed something so obvious?

For one thing, I had not really taken the word "command" to mean what it said. For example, when I thought about the Great Commission, my mind read it:

". . . teaching them to obey everything I have *taught* you."

Yet, if words mean anything (and they do), I couldn't arbitrarily substitute the word "taught" for the word "command." Now I was confronting the possibility that although Jesus had *taught* us many things, all of which are very important, He may have *commanded* us only *one* thing—to love one another as He had loved us.

As I looked again at all of the times He used the word "command"[16] in the Gospels, I discovered that Jesus applied this word uniquely to His own sayings on only two occasions. Both of these instances came after His announcement of the New Covenant. Both were recorded by the two Gospel writers who were actually present when Jesus gave His New Command—Matthew and John.[17]

Of the two unique instances when Jesus used the word "command" the first is in His final message when He gave the New

---

[15] John 15:17

[16] For more on the use of "command" (*entellomai* and *entole*) in the Gospels, see Appendix B.

[17] Whereas Matthew and John were among The Twelve, Mark and Luke were not. Many believe Mark was mentored by the Apostle Peter and Luke by the Apostle Paul.

Command to the disciples at the Last Supper.

> A new *command* I give you: Love one another. As I have
> loved you, so you must love one another.[18]

The second is when He gave His final charge—the Great Commission—to His disciples just before His ascension.

> Therefore go and make disciples of all nations, baptizing
> them in the name of the Father and of the Son and of the
> Holy Spirit, and teaching them to obey everything I have
> *commanded* you.[19]

Now I had to consider the possibility that Jesus may have used
the word "commanded" in the Great Commission to highlight the
significance of His command to love one another that He had given
only weeks earlier at the Last Supper.

It seemed reasonable to me that Jesus, in commissioning His
followers to make disciples of all the nations, would have reiterated
the importance of loving one another as He had loved them. After
all, their *love for one another* would be the mark of authenticity by
which those who were Jesus' followers would forever be identified
as His disciples!

I had started my study that morning at my kitchen table with a
question: What all *did* Jesus command His disciples to obey? That
question had led me to discover a stunning omission in my
thinking. It was the *New Commandment—His Command*.

In fact, I seemed to be more familiar with the Ten Commandments that God gave through Moses than I was with the One

---

[18] John 13:34
[19] Matthew 28:19-20

Commandment[20] that God gave through Jesus Christ, His Son. How could this be? I had attended church all my life. Yet in my training, in years of personal study and in decades of teaching others, I could not remember being taught or teaching others this basic truth. "Love one another" was Jesus' Command—the One Command He owned as "His." How could I possibly have missed something so clear, so obvious and so simple?

While I may have missed the significance of the New Commandment Jesus had given, I was certain that the early church fathers would not have overlooked it. I was sure they would have much to say about something this important.

It was to them that I would look next.

---

[20] Just as the words "Ten Commandments" given through Moses are capitalized, I have chosen to capitalize the words "One Commandment" given by Jesus.

CHAPTER 4

THE EARLY CHURCH FATHERS

The leaders of the church who came after the twelve apostles became known as the *early church fathers*. Between the years A.D. 125 to 325 they were the overseers of a rapidly growing number of Christians. They are also known as the ante-Nicene fathers. We are given a window into their thinking through 10,000 pages of their writings.

From my perspective, these men lived as close as you could get to authentic Christian faith and practice—at least after the death of the first apostles. That's why I was eager to see what these fifty or so early leaders had to say about the command that had gripped my attention. And I knew just where to look to find out what they had to say about it—Bercot's *A Dictionary of Early Christian Beliefs*.[1]

I had stumbled onto David Bercot's dictionary just a couple of months earlier as I was looking through the religious book section at Barnes & Noble. It was billed as *A Reference Guide to More Than 700 Topics Discussed by the Early Church Fathers*. Bercot had combed through the 10,000 pages they had written and catalogued the contents under 700 topics. With that many topics listed, I was sure I would strike gold when I looked up something as significant as Jesus' Commandment or the Command of Christ.

---

[1] David W. Bercot, ed., *A Dictionary of Early Christian Beliefs* (Peabody: Hendrickson, 1998).

I got up from the kitchen table to retrieve Bercot's dictionary from a tall stack of books that had accumulated on my desk over the past six months. As I settled back down at the table, I began to thumb through it, looking for Jesus' Commandment or the Command of Christ. I found CLERGY, CLOTHING, COMMUNION, CONCEPTION, but nothing on Jesus' COMMANDMENT or the COMMAND of Christ.

"Maybe it's under LAW of Christ," I thought. There was LAW of Moses, Natural LAW, Roman LAW, and LAWSUITS, but no LAW of Christ.

"What about just plain LOVE or CHARITY?" I thought to myself. It did reference Jesus' teaching about "loving our enemies," but I could find no reference to Jesus' Command *to love one another as He had loved us!*

I was stunned. I had been so sure I would find a treasure-trove of insights and applications relating to Jesus' Command from the writings of these early church leaders. But nothing?[2]

A wave of disbelief swept over me. I had started the day with a question: *What all had Jesus commanded His disciples to obey?* That question had brought me to a profound personal discovery. But now I was left with a second question: *Whatever happened to Jesus' Command?*

I had nowhere to go but back to the words that Jesus had spoken, "teaching them to obey everything I have commanded you."[3]

I carefully examined each word in His statement. The word "obey" caught my attention. Some Bible translations render it

---

[2] See Appendix C
[3] Matthew 28:20

"observe" — "teaching them to *observe* all things whatsoever I have commanded you."[4] I actually liked the word "obey" better. "Observe" is a word that on the surface seemed too casual for my taste. But in the Greek language, the word used there is *tereo*, a very powerful word that means "to guard (from loss . . . by keeping the eye upon)."[5] There is nothing casual or passive about *tereo*. It is a word that implies focus, protection and vigilance.

Suddenly, some pieces started to come together in my thinking. Jesus was saying that a central part of His assignment to His followers was to teach others *to guard—to protect from loss by never taking their eyes off*—what He had *commanded* them. Certainly that included the *New Command—His Command*—He had so recently given them.

A new command I give you: Love one another. As I have loved you, so you must love one another.[6]

My command is this: Love each other as I have loved you.[7]

This is my command: Love each other.[8]

Why do we guard something? Why did Jesus tell them to guard—to protect from loss by never taking their eyes off—what He had commanded them? He asked them to protect it from loss because it is valuable, essential, one-of-a-kind and irreplaceable. Its loss would be *catastrophic!*

A better translation of Jesus' words of commission might be: teaching them to guard—to protect by never taking their eyes off—

---

[4] Matthew 28:20 KJV
[5] James Strong, *The New Strong's Exhaustive Concordance of the Bible* (New York: Nelson, 1984).
[6] John 13:34
[7] John 15:12
[8] John 15:17

the whole of that which I commanded you.[9]

I was beginning to hypothesize why Bercot had cited no reference to Jesus' Command in the writings of the early church fathers. First, the early fathers said so little about Jesus' Command that it failed to flag his attention. Second, the New Command has been so obscured in our contemporary theology that Bercot didn't even think of it as one of the 700 topics to research.

The focus of these early fathers seems to have been drawn away from the Command by the speculative ideas and doctrines that were being promoted by unscrupulous pretenders, well-meaning believers and would-be leaders. Which of these ideas and doctrines were true, which were false and which were heresies? They had to address these questions. It was a large and unenviable challenge that these early leaders felt they could not escape. They had to preserve orthodoxy (right belief about God) and orthopraxy (right practice of the newly founded Christian faith).

To find answers and to resolve these issues, these early leaders began to communicate with one another by letter. Then they met in councils to discuss these matters and agree on right doctrine and corrective measures. Finally, they started to write creeds to ensure that the faithful would have a correct understanding of God and sound Christian doctrine.

Yet, sadly, in the quest for orthodoxy, the New Command—to love one another as Jesus had loved us—seemed to have slipped unnoticed out of their sight. Instead, their focus had been shifted to the speculative issues demanding their attention. The need to establish correct doctrine for the Christian faith had drawn their eyes off the very Command that Jesus had told them to guard—to

---

[9] My paraphrase of Matthew 28:20

protect from loss by never letting it out of their sight.

These early Christians had a treasure—the Command given them by Jesus. They loved each other deeply. This love was clearly seen in the scriptural record of those early years.

> All the believers were together and had everything in common. Selling their possessions and goods, they gave to anyone as he had need. Every day they continued to meet together in the temple courts. They broke bread in their homes and ate together with glad and sincere hearts, praising God and enjoying the favor of all the people. And the Lord added to their number daily those who were being saved.[10]

However, with the passage of time, their love for one another was tested. Over the decades that followed, it appears that their attention drifted from the Command Jesus had given them.[11]

Beyond that, it was as if a master thief was lurking in the shadows. He had spotted the treasure and he hated it. If only he could steal their mark of authenticity! All he needed was for them to take their eyes off the Command so he could slip it away.

It seems that this thief was willing to let them have orthodoxy, but only if defined *without* the One Command Jesus had given them. Let them debate their doctrines, disagree with one another, even ignore and dislike each other. He would keep them so preoccupied in their quest for sound doctrine that they wouldn't even miss the stolen treasure. His wildest scheme was that they would come to hate each other—better yet, kill one another—in their quest to preserve an incomplete orthodoxy!

---

[10] Acts 2:44-47
[11] See Revelation 2:4-5

Thus, a core commandment of Christian discipleship faded from the vision of the early church fathers. The unfortunate irony is that the goal of orthodoxy was to keep Christianity authentic. Yet the very mark of authenticity that Jesus had given them was lost, even as they pursued this noble goal.

It was now late afternoon, May 1, 2002. After the debilitating crisis I had experienced, it was great to have recovered enough to study the Bible again. But I felt like Someone *really big* had taken me by the ankles, turned me upside down and shaken a lot of personal, theological change out of my pockets.

I had started the day with a question: What all *had* Jesus commanded His disciples to obey? And in seeking an answer to that question, I had been confronted with a stunning omission in my thinking. Although Jesus had taught us many things, He had clearly commanded us *one thing*. It was the New Command—His Command.

My command is this: Love each other as I have loved you.[12]

I could no longer overlook Jesus' Command. In fact, it seemed impossible to overestimate its value or overemphasize its significance. It had to be a *core commandment* of authentic Christianity.

I had no idea how profoundly this understanding would transform my daily journey of Christian faith and practice. Like finding a missing piece in a puzzle, my personal discovery of Jesus' Command began to make the picture complete for me.

When this piece was put into place, I was able to see how clearly it fit with another foundational truth of authentic Christianity, one

---

[12] John 15:12

that had faired much better over the centuries than the Command that Jesus had given us.

It was on these two core commandments that I would next focus.

CHAPTER 5

TWO CORE COMMANDMENTS

Over the next few weeks, I was amazed to discover how clearly Jesus' Command was connected with another well-known tenant of Christianity—God's command that we believe in Jesus Christ. Together, these two were emerging in my thinking as *the core commandments* of authentic Christianity. This new understanding was powerfully reinforced in my mind by the words of John the apostle in his first letter.

> This is His [God's] commandment, that we [1] believe in
> the name of His Son Jesus Christ, and [2] love one another,
> just as He [Jesus] commanded us.[1]

When I looked more closely at this statement, it became clear that God, seen here as Father, commanded that we "believe in the name of His Son, Jesus Christ." This was God's command to us. Then Jesus Christ, God's Son, commanded that we "love one another." John intentionally linked these two commands. Together, they are the *two core commandments* of authentic Christian faith and practice.

Although these two core commandments were new to me, it quickly became apparent that they weren't new to the writers of the New Testament. Consider the following passages from the letters:

---

[1] 1 John 3:23 NAS

LETTER TO THE COLOSSIANS

We always thank God, the Father of our Lord Jesus Christ, when we pray for you, because we have heard [1] of your *faith* in Christ Jesus and [2] of the *love* you have for all the saints.[2]

LETTER TO THE EPHESIANS

For this reason, ever since I heard about [1] your *faith* in the Lord Jesus and [2] your *love* for all the saints, I have not stopped giving thanks for you, remembering you in my prayers.[3]

LETTER TO PHILEMON

I always thank my God as I remember you in my prayers, because I hear about [1] your *faith* in the Lord Jesus and [2] your *love* for all the saints.[4]

LETTER TO THE GALATIANS

For in Christ Jesus neither circumcision nor uncircumcision has any value. The only thing that counts is [1] *faith* expressing itself [2] through *love*.[5]

LETTER TO THE HEBREWS

Let us draw near with a true heart in [1] full assurance of *faith*. . . . And let us consider one another in order to [2] stir up *love* and good works.[6]

One of the most insightful uses of these two core commands

---

[2] Colossians 1:3-4
[3] Ephesians 1:15-16
[4] Philemon 1:4-5
[5] Galatians 5:6
[6] Hebrews 10:22, 24 NKJV

was found in the story of Paul and his friends in the city of Thessalonica.

In short, Paul, Silas and Timothy were on their second missionary journey when they arrived in Thessalonica.[7] Paul went to the local synagogue where, for three Sabbaths in a row, he taught that Jesus was the promised Messiah, that He was crucified and raised from the dead. A significant number of people believed what he was teaching. Then trouble broke out, and their host was arrested. That night, Paul and his company were smuggled out of the city and made a hasty getaway under the cover of darkness.

Apparently, Paul could not get these newfound friends, now believers in Jesus Christ, off his mind. He decided to send Timothy to visit them and bring back word about how they were doing. Upon Timothy's return, Paul writes his first letter to them. In it, he explains that he missed them so much that he had sent Timothy on the long journey to find out how they were doing.

> But Timothy has just now come to us from you and has brought good news about your [1] faith and [2] love.[8]

Why did Paul say "good news about your faith and love"? My original thinking was that Paul was commending their faith in God and love for God. However, my understanding was amended when I read his second letter to them, written only months later. As he opens his second letter, Paul writes the following:

> We ought always to thank God for you . . . because [1] your faith is growing more and more, and [2] the love every one of you *has for each other* is increasing.[9]

---

[7] See Acts 17:1-9

[8] 1 Thessalonians 3:6

[9] 2 Thessalonians 1:3

It was becoming clear to me that (1) faith in Jesus Christ and (2) love for one another were indeed recognized by the writers of the New Testament as marks of authenticity. Whenever they found these two expressions of grace in people, they took them to be signs of the new life that was promised to those who put their faith in Jesus Christ.

GOOD NEWS/BAD NEWS

I was now confronted with a very real good news/bad news scenario. The good news was this: The *first core commandment*—God's command that we believe in His Son, Jesus Christ—has been taught as a central truth for much of Christian history.

The bad news was that although early Christians loved one another deeply, history revealed the astonishing and early loss of the *second core commandment*—Jesus' Command that we love one another as He has loved us.

After finding no reference to Jesus' Command in Bercot's *Dictionary*, I started my own search of the writings of the early church fathers. Indeed, references that specifically focused on Jesus' Command were rare between the years A.D. 125-325. Out of fifty early fathers whose writings remain, I found only two that made direct reference to it, Clement of Alexandria and Cyprian of Carthage. Clement made one specific reference to the Command and Cyprian of Carthage made four direct references to it.

Here is one of Cyprian's four references:

Discord cannot attain to the kingdom of heaven; to the rewards of Christ, who said, "This is my commandment that ye love one another even as I have loved you." He cannot attain who has violated the love of Christ by faithless dissension. He who has not charity has not God.[10]

In another treatise, Cyprian wrote these words:

But what did the Lord more frequently instill into His disciples, what did He more charge to be guarded and observed among His saving counsels and heavenly precepts, than that with the same love wherewith He Himself loved the disciples, we also should love one another?[11]

Beginning in the second century, creeds, catechisms and formal confessions of faith became increasingly important in teaching the doctrines of Christianity. Some of the more well-known ones include the Apostles' Creed (third century), the Nicene Creed (325), the Heidelberg Catechism (1563) and the Westminster Confession of Faith (1646). Unfortunately, *none of these contains a reference to Jesus' Command to love one another.* In fact, the words "love one another" are strangely absent from all of these creeds and confessions. Rather, emphasis was increasingly placed on the Old Testament commandments. In large part, Jesus' Command disappeared from Christian teaching. *For all practical purposes, it was lost!*

As I pondered my personal discovery of Jesus' Command, it was evident that I had a lot to learn. I did see that it was clearly linked with God's Command that we believe in His Son, Jesus Christ. For the first time, I was seeing faith in Jesus Christ and love for one another as the *two core commandments* of historic Christianity. And I was seeing, not only the significance of His Command, but also the consequences of its loss.

The adventure would only deepen in the months ahead.

---

[10] Cyprian, "On the Unity of the Church," in *The Ante-Nicene Fathers,* Vol 5, eds. A. Roberts and J. Donaldson (Albany: AGES Digital Library, 1997), 874.

[11] Cyprian, "On Jealousy and Envy," in *The Ante-Nicene Fathers,* Vol 5, eds. A. Roberts and J. Donaldson (Albany: AGES Digital Library, 1997), 1010.

CHAPTER 6

YOU CAN ASK A QUESTION

My yearlong season of recovery was now over, and I was back with the congregation I had served for thirty-three years. By this time, I knew that my role as senior pastor was coming to an end, and I was working to help position the congregation for a future without me.

My discovery of Jesus' Command was having a profound impact on me. I had become fully persuaded that believing in Jesus and guarding the Command He had given was at the heart of true Christian discipleship. But at the same time, some doubt had begun to gnaw away at the joy of this newfound understanding. I was torn between the One New Command I was now seeing and the two commandments I had always believed best summarized the Christian faith.

I had believed and taught for many years that Jesus' Command was, "Love the Lord your God with all your heart and with all your soul and with all your mind . . . [and] love your neighbor as yourself."[1] But now I had clearly seen His Command, stated five times in His final message to the disciples.

A new command I give you: *Love one another.* As I have

---

[1] Matthew 22:37, 39

loved you, so you must *love one another*. By this all men will know that you are my disciples, if you *love one another*.[2]

My command is this: *Love each other* as I have loved you.[3]

This is my command: *Love each other*.[4]

I found myself thinking, "If only Jesus had said, 'These are my *two* commandments: Love the Lord your God with all your heart and with all your soul and with all your mind, and love one another as I have loved you.' That would be much easier for me to accept!"

I even wondered if Jesus had in some way compro . . . I couldn't even say it in my head, for to say it would be to acknowledge that I doubted my Lord Jesus! Every time the thought would attempt to surface, I would stuff it back into the corner of my mind, hoping that such an irreverent idea would not come to the attention of my Lord.

But then on a February morning in 2003, I awakened with a special sense of God's nearness. It was as if He had been whispering to me as I slept and awakened me with the words, "You can ask a question."

Immediately I was aware that I did have a question, one that had been quietly demanding a hearing for months. To me the invitation to ask revealed that the inviter knew the question already, so I simply let it surface without attempting to cover it up.

How could Jesus give us only one command—to love one another as He had loved us—and not include loving God first?

There. I'd said it.

---

[2] John 13:34-35
[3] John 15:12
[4] John 15:17

GOD'S NEW HOME

As I lay quietly on my bed in the minutes that followed, a stream of thoughts and Scriptures came flooding into my mind.

The first thing that I became aware of was that when Jesus gave us the New Command, He knew something we didn't know. (That may be the largest understatement in this book!) He fully knew the nature of the New Covenant that He had just introduced and would enact only hours later when He was crucified. He would die on the cross and be buried. On the third day, He would be raised from the dead.

Moreover, He fully understood that in this New Covenant, God would, for the first time in human history, come to live *in* those who believed in Him. Without a doubt, God had been *with* His covenant people in the past—in the cloud and pillar of fire, the Ark of the Covenant and the magnificent Temple. He had also come upon them. But now He would make His home *in* His people.

I remembered that when He introduced the New Command, Jesus spoke these words to His disciples: "And I will ask the Father, and he will give you another Counselor to be with you forever—the Spirit of truth. . . . You know him, for he lives *with* you and *will be in you*."[5]

He continued by saying, "If anyone loves me, he will obey my teaching. My Father will love him, and *we will come to him* and *make our home with him*."[6]

This astonishing reality was underlined in New Testament Scripture. In his first letter to the Corinthian believers, Paul the

---

[5] John 14:16-17
[6] John 14:23

apostle said, "Don't you know that you yourselves are *God's temple* and that *God's Spirit lives in you*?"[7]

In his second letter, Paul continued, ". . . for *ye are a sanctuary of the living God*, according as God said—'I will dwell *in*[8] them, and will walk among [them], and I will be their God, and they shall be My people.' "[9]

Paul saw this as a very important part of the message God had sent him to deliver. He was bringing the answer to a "mystery that has been kept hidden for ages and generations, but is now disclosed to the saints . . . which is Christ *in you*, the hope of glory."[10]

As I lay on my bed, God was reminding me that because He now lived *in* those people who believed in Jesus, we would need to love Him in His place of dwelling—*in* those people who believed in Him. He was making Himself accessible to us *in* our brothers and sisters, but it would be impossible to love Him *in* them if we did not *love the brothers and sisters in whom He now lived!* It was only when we hugged them that God would feel the squeeze!

MUST ALSO LOVE HIS BROTHER

The second thing that came to my mind was the following words of Scripture:

> If anyone says, "I love God," yet hates his brother, he is a liar. For anyone who does not love his brother, whom he has seen, cannot love God, whom he has not seen. And he has given us this command: Whoever loves God must also

---

[7] 1 Corinthians 3:16
[8] *Enoikeo*—to inhabit (*Strong's New Exhaustive Concordance* with Expanded Greek-Hebrew Dictionary)
[9] 2 Corinthians 6:16 *Young's Literal Translation*
[10] Colossians 1:26-27

love his brother.[11]

In that moment, it seemed even clearer to me that God was deliberately positioning Himself so we could *only* love Him as we love our brothers and sisters *in whom He now lives.* If I don't love my brothers and sisters, it is impossible to "get to God" in order to love Him.

The words "cannot love God" seemed extremely significant to me in that moment. More important than my screaming toward the stars in the night sky, "I LOVE YOU, GOD!"—He was asking me to love my brothers and my sisters who were standing right next to me on planet earth. In so doing *I would be loving Him, too, as He now made His home in them.*

YOU VISITED ME

Yet a third account from Scripture flooded my mind. Jesus was having a question-and-answer session with His disciples on the Mount of Olives.

The dialogue started when the disciples called His attention to the impressive structure of the Temple in Jerusalem. Jesus responded by telling them that the building of which they were in awe would soon be destroyed. That led them to ask a question: "When will this happen, and what will be the sign of your coming and of the end of the age?"[12]

As His answer unfolded, He told of a time when He would return as King and peoples' ultimate destinies would be revealed.

When the Son of Man comes in his glory . . . he will separate the people one from another as a shepherd separates the sheep from the goats. He will put the sheep

---

[11] 1 John 4:20-21
[12] Matthew 24:3

on his right and the goats on his left.

Then the King will say to those on his right, "Come, you who are blessed by my Father; take your inheritance, the kingdom prepared for you since the creation of the world. For I was hungry and you gave me something to eat, I was thirsty and you gave me something to drink, I was a stranger and you invited me in, I needed clothes and you clothed me, I was sick and you looked after me, I was in prison and you came to visit me."

Then the righteous will answer him, "Lord, *when* did we see you hungry and feed you, or thirsty and give you something to drink? *When* did we see you a stranger and invite you in, or needing clothes and clothe you? *When* did we see you sick or in prison and go to visit you?"

The King will reply, "I tell you the truth, *whatever you did for one of the least of these brothers of mine, you did for me."*[13]

Lying there in those moments, I was struck by the strength of His identification with His brothers and sisters, His New Covenant family—even the least of them. His identity as *being in them* was stronger than I had ever imagined. A closer look at what Jesus is saying reveals that I wasn't alone in my surprise.

The response of the righteous will be something like this: "Lord, I don't remember even *seeing You*, let alone *seeing You* hungry, thirsty, lonely, needy, sick or imprisoned! How could I possibly have fed, clothed or visited You?"

It's as if Jesus were saying, "Don't you remember that I promised to make My home in those who trust in Me? Every act of love that you did to your brothers and sisters, *you were actually doing to Me*. I was living right there inside of them."

---

[13] Matthew 25:31-40

This truth was affirmed in the New Testament letter to the Hebrews:

> For God is not unjust. He will not forget how hard you have worked for him and how *you have shown your love to him by caring for other believers,* as you still do. Our great desire is that you will keep on loving others as long as life lasts. . . . Then you will not become spiritually dull and indifferent.[14]

One final image came flooding into my mind in those moments. It was a picture of me a few months earlier standing at our kitchen range scrambling eggs.

That's a story all its own.

---

[14] Hebrews 6:10-12 NLT

CHAPTER 7

A BREAKFAST SURPRISE

One morning about eight months into my recovery, I was preparing breakfast for my wife. Patti was sitting behind me at the kitchen table, and I was standing at the range. I had just cracked a couple of eggs into a small mixing bowl and was preparing to blend them with a spoonful of cottage cheese. At that instant, I was surprised by a very clear whisper: "Jesus came to your house for breakfast today."

It was that clear, that short and that simple. The tone of the voice was not abrupt or sharp. It was subdued, not drawing attention to the messenger, but rather to the information that I needed to hear.

When I heard the whisper, I stopped swirling the fork in the bowl of unscrambled eggs and stood motionless. Tears began to fill my eyes. The message was clear. In the stillness of that moment, I was fully aware that only one person was sitting at the table behind me waiting for breakfast. It was my wife. Yet in that same instant, I knew that I was about to scramble eggs for Jesus.

Moments passed. As the tears began to clear from my eyes, I scrambled the eggs and then poured them into the waiting skillet. The toast popped up as I was turning the eggs for the final time. I slid them onto a plate and buttered the toast. With the breakfast in my hand, I took the half-dozen steps from the range to our kitchen table. Patti looked up in anticipation of the steaming scrambled eggs and warm toast. I put the plate in front of her.

"Here's breakfast, Babe. Can I get you anything else? Water? Juice?"

In that moment, it was clear to me that if I ever wanted to serve Jesus breakfast, I would never have a better opportunity.

It didn't happen overnight, but by the time a couple of months had passed, my attitude in serving my wife had changed. Let me explain.

BREAKFAST THE WAY IT WAS BEFORE

About four years after Patti and I were married, she was diagnosed with hypoglycemia, commonly known as low blood sugar. To me, it was helpful information. It explained why she would experience periodic waves of weakness. All her energy would seem to disappear, only to reappear a few hours later.

As the years progressed, I remained vaguely aware of the problem that Patti was experiencing. I say "vaguely aware" because by that time I was fully engaged as the senior pastor of a growing church.

Those words, "growing church," had a special significance to me. I had been willing to pay the price in early morning prayer, endless breakfast and lunch appointments, and meetings with key leaders and committees. In addition to weddings and funerals, there were my weekend responsibilities of overseeing multiple Sunday services and giving the sermon that was to inspire and nourish all those who were members of my congregation. (I will spare you the building programs and meetings with architects, city officials, planning commissions and government agencies.) It was hard work, yet very fulfilling. Being a successful pastor was keeping me occupied, challenged and excited!

It was during this busy season of successful ministry that my wife started to call me from time to time late in the morning.

"I am so weak. Can you bring me something to eat?"

"Honey, what would you like? What can I bring you?"

"I don't know. I . . . I can't think. Anything!"

I loved Patti. I tried to be understanding. However, I was a very busy person. I didn't know if she fully understood how difficult it was for me to juggle appointments so I could respond to these interrup— . . . uh . . . calls for help. Yet being a good pastor, a good husband, a good father, a good neighbor, a good citizen, a good everything was very important to me.

As Patti was eating the hamburger I had brought her, I would start the lecture.

"What did you have for breakfast?"

"I wasn't hungry when I got up. I didn't eat anything."

"You know that you have to eat some breakfast or your blood sugar will drop!"

"I know, but I didn't have any appetite when I got up!"

This was repeated with increasing frequency over a period of months until a thought came to my mind. I controlled my own schedule. I got up very early, was out of the house and at work before Patti was awake. What if I arranged my work schedule so I could come back to the house at about 9:00 in the morning? I could cook breakfast for Patti, take some time to connect with her and then continue with the rest of my day.

It worked. Patti appreciated my coming home and having some time with her in the morning. She was glad to eat a couple of eggs with a slice of toast if I fixed it for her. Making breakfast was easy for me. It doesn't take long to scramble a couple of eggs and toast a slice of bread.

Just this simple change turned out to be good for both of us. It gave me some time to connect with my wife in the morning. It helped Patti get her day started right. Most of the time, I did this new breakfast routine with a pretty good attitude. Now and then, however, I would feel pressured, taken advantage of or inconvenienced because of having to break into my schedule to make her breakfast. On those days, I could feel the tension in my face as I slid the plate of eggs and toast across the table.

"Can I get you anything else, Honey?"

"Could I have some jam for my toast?"

"Sure."

I was doing and saying the right things, only sometimes I had to squeeze the words out between my teeth because my jaw seemed reluctant to open.

But after that breakfast and hearing the words "Jesus came to your house for breakfast today," things began changing for me.

It wasn't just an emotion; it was the recognition that I had the privilege of serving breakfast to Jesus! I even took out the kitchen garbage for Him a number of times when it was overflowing.

Months passed before I told Patti what had happened to me that morning. In fact, it was not until I felt I was ready to share it publicly that I told her about making Jesus breakfast that day. Now she says it's one of the best messages she's ever heard me preach; she loves to hear me share it. Come to think of it, a lot of women seem to like that message.

I was beginning to see how practical the truth really was about God living in people of faith! When I treated them with love, I was treating Him with love. And when I treated them carelessly and with indifference, I was treating Him carelessly and with indifference. This was becoming a clear reality to me as I was seeing the significance of Jesus' Command—to love one another as He has loved us.

The sobering prophetic words that Jesus had given His disciples were now speaking to me as never before.

> I tell you the truth, whatever you did for one of the least of these brothers of mine, you did for me. . . . [And] whatever you did not do for one of the least of these, you did not do for me.[1]

Two amazing truths were becoming clear: (1) Unless I loved my brothers and sisters, I could not love God, and (2) when I loved my brothers and sisters, I could not help but love God, too!

GOD'S LOVE LANGUAGE

In the 1990s, Patti had asked me to read *The Five Love Languages*, by Gary Chapman.[2] The book gives a very insightful description of five ways we receive love from others: words of affirmation, quality time, gifts, acts of service and physical touch. He says that for each of us, one of these is our primary love language—the way we most naturally receive love.

Patti realized that her primary love language is quality time. My primary love language is words of affirmation. As Chapman points out, sometimes we miss effectively communicating our love to another because we don't "speak" in the language our loved one best understands.

---

[1] Matthew 25:40, 45

[2] Gary D. Chapman, *The Five Love Languages* (Chicago: Northfield, 1992).

He is right. Many times, I had missed communicating my love to Patti in the language she understood best—quality time.

In the New Covenant, loving God is as important as it ever was. But how does He best receive our expressions of love? Is it sacrifices and offerings that God wants? Is He waiting to hear words of adoration from us? If so, I could spend hours shouting into the sky, "I love You, God! You are awesome!"

I think that words of affirmation mean something to God, kind of like when your five-year-old child draws a picture of a heart on construction paper and then asks you to tell him the letters of the alphabet that spell "i LOve yUO." It's really special! However, there comes a point in parenting when we say to our precious little (or big) children, "If you love Mommy (or Daddy), obey me when I tell you not to hit your sister. Treat her nicely!"

I think that's what God is saying when He commands us to believe in His Son, Jesus Christ, and listen to Him. When we believe in Jesus and listen to Him, we hear His Command: "My command is this: Love each other as I have loved you."[3]

To me, it seems the way God best receives love from us is through our *obedience* to Him. When we obey His Command to love one another, we give God a double hug—the hug of obedience and then the hug He feels when we love those in whom He now makes His home. Because God now lives in those who believe in Jesus, He can't help but feel the squeeze when we love one another.

So rather than shouting "I love You, God!" into the sky for hours, I began to realize that maybe I should give just a couple of shouts and then go back into the kitchen and help my wife clean up the pots and pans after dinner. Then I could give her some quality time. I would be speaking *God's love language* and communicating

---

[3] John 15:12

my deep love for Him through my simple obedience to His command. Of course, Patti would feel loved and special, too!

My question, "How could Jesus give us only one command?" had been answered. In the New Covenant, loving God and loving our neighbors are expressed as we put our faith in Jesus Christ and love one another.

With that new understanding, it seemed important that I clearly grasp the difference between the Old Covenant based on the Law of Moses and the New Covenant based on Jesus' Command.

I would look into that next.

CHAPTER 8

COMPARING THE OLD AND NEW

In my present ministry, I'm often asked the question, "What do you do?" I explain that I work with pastors and emerging leaders and that I'm writing a book. Many times the next question is, "What is the book about?" I tell them that I'm writing about the Command Jesus gave us. Often there is a brief pause and then a follow-up question: "Which command?"

That's a great question. For many Christians, Jesus' Command is "Love God with all your heart, soul and mind and love your neighbor as yourself." When I informally survey Christian congregations, more than half of them give this as their answer. I certainly understand their response.

Many times Jesus taught using parables, stories designed to get a point across. Sometimes the lesson was hidden within the story so that only those asking a follow-up question could get the answer. But there was one thing Jesus made very clear—His Command. He announced it in the clearest terms and then repeated it two more times on the night He gave it.

A new command I give you: Love one another. As I have loved you, so you must love one another.[1]

---

[1] John 13:34

My command is this: Love each other as I have loved you.[2]

This is my command: Love each other.[3]

Yet, astonishingly, in my experience only about one in ten Christians gives that as their answer! Most of us, and I was one, have substituted the two core commandments of the Old Covenant in place of the two core commandments of the New Covenant. In so doing, we crowd out the Command Jesus gave us. But how did we come to think this way?

To find the answer to that question, I needed to take a closer look at the Old and New Testaments and the covenants and commandments they contained. First, I turned my attention to the Old Testament. For many, it is best known for the Ten Commandments, the ones written by God in stone and handed to Moses on Mount Sinai. For Orthodox Jews, the Old Testament contains 613 commandments recorded in the Torah.

Are some of these commandments more significant than others? Apparently, Jesus thought so. One day an expert in the Law of Moses came to Him with a question:

Teacher, which is the greatest commandment in the Law?[4]

Jesus answered him:

"Love the Lord your God with all your heart and with all your soul and with all your mind." This is the first and greatest commandment. And the second is like it: "Love your neighbor as yourself." All the Law and the Prophets

---

[2] John 15:12
[3] John 15:17
[4] Matthew 22:36

hang on these two commandments.[5]

In giving him this answer, Jesus summarized the two core commandments *of the Old Testament.* These provide us with significant insight into the covenant that existed at that time. But that covenant would soon be made *old* by the introduction of the long-promised *New* Covenant.

All that Jesus was, said and did converged when He introduced the New Covenant and gave us the New Commandment at the Last Supper. The *new* was enacted in the hours that followed, through Jesus' death and resurrection and a fresh infusion of the Holy Spirit. These realities are foundational to the Christian faith.

I knew that although "the law was given through Moses; *grace* and *truth* came through Jesus Christ."[6] In this New Covenant, we are "not under law, but under *grace.*"[7] As one who now lives in the New Covenant and under *grace,* what if I asked Jesus a question similar to the one asked by the previously mentioned expert in the Law of Moses? If I did, that question would sound something like this: "Teacher, what is the greatest commandment for those living in grace and truth?"

Actually, I saw that Jesus had answered that question in two parts. The first half was given when He answered a question asked by someone in a crowd: "What must we do to do the works God requires?"[8]

For most of the people in the crowd, the way to be righteous and to please God was through works, obeying all of the commandments contained in the Law of Moses. Yet Jesus' answer was

---

[5] Matthew 22:37-40
[6] John 1:17
[7] Romans 6:14
[8] John 6:28

surprisingly different. He said, "The work of God is this: to *believe* in the one he has sent."[9]

This is the *first core commandment* of Christianity. *Believing* in Jesus is at the heart of the New Covenant. Putting our trust in Him is where the Christian faith starts. Again, this is underscored when He spoke the *first core commandment* of the New Covenant in these familiar words:

> For God so loved the world that he gave his one and only Son, that whoever *believes* in him shall not perish but have eternal life.[10]

Later, Jesus gave us the *second core commandment* of the New Covenant:

> A new command I give you: *Love* one another. As I have *loved* you, so you must *love* one another. By this all men will know that you are my disciples, if you *love* one another.[11]

These two core commandments of the New Covenant are expressed most succinctly in the words of John the apostle in his first letter:

> We have confidence before God . . . because we obey his commands and do what pleases him. And this is his command: [1] to *believe* in the name of his Son, Jesus Christ, and [2] to *love* one another as he commanded us.[12]

God, as the Father, commanded us *to believe in His Son*. Jesus, as God's Son, commanded us *to love one another*. Together, these are the

---

[9] John 6:29
[10] John 3:16
[11] John 13:34-35
[12] 1 John 3:21-23

core commandments of the New Covenant and of the Christian faith.

Now I recognized that both the Old Testament and the New Testament had core commandments. Yet I had never seen them side-by-side. For the first time, I placed them next to each other. When I did this, I could clearly see significant differences between the two.

Core Commandments of the Old Covenant	Core Commandments of the New Covenant
(1) "Love the LORD your God with all your heart and with all your soul and with all your strength." Deuteronomy 6:5	(1) "For God so loved the world that he gave his one and only Son, that whoever believes in him shall not perish but have eternal life." John 3:16
(2) "Love your neighbor as yourself." Leviticus 19:18	(2) "Love one another. As I have loved you, so you must love one another." John 13:34

As I read them side-by-side, I faced the question: Does it matter which of these core commandments I identify as applying most directly to me? I realized, both from Scripture and from personal experience, that it does. The two core commandments of the Old Covenant are rooted in *my finite ability* to love God and my neighbor.

1. Love the LORD your God with all *your* heart and with all

your soul and with all *your* strength.[13]

2. Love your neighbor *as yourself.*[14]

In contrast, I realized with striking clarity that the two core commandments of the New Covenant are rooted in *God's infinite love* for me.

1. For *God so loved* the world that he gave his one and only Son, that whoever believes in him shall not perish but have eternal life.[15]

2. *As I have loved you*, so you must love one another.[16]

Jesus' words "as I have loved you" are very important in understanding the second core commandment in the New Covenant. It was the love Jesus received from His Father that enabled Him to love us: "As the Father has loved me, so have I loved you. Now remain in my love."[17] Only as I remain in His love am I empowered to love others.

In his first letter, John the apostle makes this important point very clear when he writes, "This is love: not that we loved God, but that he loved us and sent his Son as an atoning sacrifice for our sins. . . . We love because he first loved us."[18]

I was now seeing a very significant difference between the Old and the New Covenants. The Old Covenant is rooted in my finite love for Him and my finite love for my neighbor; the New Covenant is rooted in God's infinite love for me.

---

[13] Deuteronomy 6:5
[14] Leviticus 19:18
[15] John 3:16
[16] John 13:34
[17] John 15:9
[18] 1 John 4:10, 19

For many years, I had believed in Jesus Christ and the New Covenant He enacted. Yet I had made the core commandments of the Old Testament the core commandments of my Christian faith: "Love the Lord your God with all your heart and with all your soul and with all your mind and with all your strength . . . [and] love your neighbor as yourself."[19]

As a result of this, I struggled with a nagging sense that I wasn't really living up to what God expected from me. My responsibilities as a husband, father, son, friend and pastor kept me from being as devoted to God as I felt I should be.

This was my struggle: If I love God with *all* my heart, *all* my soul, *all* my mind and *all* my strength, does that leave *any* of my heart, soul, mind or strength with which to love others?

For years, I subconsciously answered that question: "No, not if I'm doing it right!" I answered no because *some* of my heart, soul, mind and strength was being diverted to other things—my wife, my children and people around me.

"I should be spending *more time* in prayer and in the study of Scripture," I thought. "I need to be doing the things that *really show* my love for God!"

From there, it was easy to wrongly assume that whatever part of my love I reserved for others and for myself was the measure of my personal failure to love God fully. I felt I disappointed (if not displeased) God when I saved some of that love for myself or others.

But then I saw the New Command that Jesus gave us:

A new command I give you: Love one another. As I have loved you, so you must love one another. By this all men

---

[19] Mark 12:30-31

will know that you are my disciples, if you love one
another.[20]

As I said earlier, this was confusing for me at first. The tension
between trying to "love God with *all*" and trying to "love one
another like I have loved you" was like attempting to drive my car
while pressing the brake and accelerator at the same time!

Once again, I looked at the question-and-answer exchange between the expert in the Law of Moses and Jesus:

> One of them [a Pharisee], an expert in the law, tested him
> with this question: "Teacher, which is the greatest com-
> mandment in the Law?"
>
> Jesus replied: " 'Love the Lord your God with all your
> heart and with all your soul and with all your mind.' This
> is the first and greatest commandment. And the second is
> like it: 'Love your neighbor as yourself.' All the Law and
> the Prophets hang on these two commandments."[21]

Following are a few of the thoughts that helped me put in
perspective Jesus' answer to the question about "the greatest
commandment in the Law."

First, Jesus was giving these words in answer to a question
about the *Law of Moses* and the covenant that existed at that time.
The man asking the question was an expert in the *Law of Moses*.
Jesus let him know that His two-part answer summed up all the
commandments found in the *Law and Prophets*.

Second, Jesus' two-part answer was not original to Him nor was
it being spoken for the first time. As recorded in Luke's Gospel

---

[20] John 13:34-35
[21] Matthew 22:35-40

account, this two-part answer had already been spoken by a man[22] who was talking with Jesus. Although it is not likely that this answer was new to this expert in the Law, it was the correct answer and one that may have already been accepted by the Jewish sect known as the Pharisees.

Third, Jesus never said that the answer He gave was His Command. If He had wanted us to embrace His two-part answer as *His Command*, He could have easily taken this opportunity to communicate that to His disciples.

Fourth, Jesus never repeated this answer again in any of His teachings. He merely answered the Pharisee's question about the Law and then moved on to other teachings.

Fifth, Jesus' two-part answer about the Law is not found in any of the New Testament Scriptures that followed. From its absence, it seems apparent that Jesus' disciples did not take His answer about the Law of Moses as one that should be repeated often and integrated into their New Covenant teaching.

Does that make "loving God" and "loving your neighbor" insignificant? Absolutely not! Jesus came to fulfill the Law. In the New Covenant, loving God is as important as it ever was! So is loving your neighbor.

Love for God has always been expressed by obedience to His commandments. In the New Covenant, we are free to love God with *all* our heart, soul, mind and strength by obeying the Father's Command to believe in His Son and by obeying His Son's Command to love one another.

These core commandments of the New Covenant—(1) *faith* in

---

[22] See Luke 10:27

Jesus Christ and (2) *love* for one another—only heighten our expression of love for God and for our neighbor. They fulfill and exceed the requirements of the Law given to Moses. Our obedience to them provides a clear and practical expression of our love for God and for our neighbor.

A HANDS-ON EXAMPLE

While I was working on this book, Patti and I stayed in the home of friends in Malibu while they were away on a short family vacation. Every morning I'd get up early to write. One day, after writing for hours, I set my laptop aside and picked up a copy of the *Los Angeles Times*. The lead story in the second section was about life in a monastery in the high desert in Southern California. The article quoted the leader of the monastery.

> We are here to have a quiet life and unite with God; there is no other reason to be here. I came because I felt I was distracted. I could not concentrate on the verse in the Bible that says you are to love the Lord your God with all your heart, all your soul and all your mind.[23]

The reporter continued by writing, "The monks . . . focus entirely on worship, not on themselves or their surroundings. They pray for hours each day, reciting vast portions of Scripture from memory and endlessly repenting of their sins."

Although I can certainly identify with the monks' struggles, the leader's words illustrate the dilemma that confronts a follower of Jesus who embraces the core commandments of the Law of Moses rather than the core commandments of the New Covenant. Attempts to love God with *all* our heart can move us toward

---

[23] David Kelly, *Los Angeles Times*, Monday, July 3, 2006, pp. B1, 10.

isolation rather than into loving relationship with the larger family of believers.

It is impossible to make the core commandments from the Law of Moses the governing rule for Christian faith without displacing the core commandments of the New Covenant. Attempting to live by the core commandments of the Old Covenant actually creates a tension that can move us away from loving one another. The antidote is for us to fully embrace the core commandments of the New Covenant—faith in Jesus Christ and love for one another.

For that to happen, we need to "make room on the table" for them. I have to recognize that the New Covenant and the Law of Christ fulfill the Old Covenant and the Law of Moses. Nothing is lost. Rather, what God has always desired is now fully realized in Jesus Christ and in those who trust in Him and obey His Command.

If you have personally trusted in Jesus as your Savior and Lord, God now makes His home in you. I encourage you then to reverently release the former Covenant. Take your foot off the brake pedal! Instead, fully embrace the New Covenant, the one enacted by your Lord and Savior, Jesus Christ. Trust Him completely! Love one another deeply with His love! In so doing, you are obeying the Father's Command that we believe in His Son and His Son's Command that we love one another as He loves us.

Personally, I now find that loving God and loving people flow much more seamlessly through both quiet and busy times, through times alone and with others. Prayer and thanksgiving are less measured by the minute. Rather, the dialogue of prayer and praise starts when I awaken to the new day and ends when I fall asleep at night.

My expressions of love for God are woven through God-and-me

times and through God-and-us times with my brothers and sisters. Prayer and praise range from silent whispers of the heart to loud cries of desperation, from spontaneous speech to carefully written verse. It's the closest I've come to prayer "without ceasing."[24]

I was personally feeling the benefits of living under the New Covenant with its New Commands. But what did the Bible have to say about why it was necessary that a New Covenant replace the Old?

That was the question I would consider next.

---

[24] See 1 Thessalonians 5:17 KJV

CHAPTER 9

THE TIME IS COMING

If I were going to understand the significance of the New Covenant, it would be helpful for me to have a clearer perspective on why there was even a need for this change. Wasn't the existing Old Covenant good enough? As I went back into the Old Testament Scriptures, the answer became clear: apparently not. Through His prophet Jeremiah, God promised a New Covenant, and it was the coming of the *new* that made the existing covenant *old* or "obsolete,"[1] as the writer of Hebrews put it.

The story of the Old Covenant is found in a body of writing known to the Hebrew people as the Torah, or Law. Christians know these same writings as the first five books[2] of the Old Testament and, along with the rest of the Bible, believe them to be sacred Scripture, inspired by God.

The Old Testament introduces God as the Creator. It tells of God's desire for relationship with the people He created. It also records special promises God made to Abraham, a man known for his amazing journey from Ur of the Chaldeans (Iraq today) to a land that God said, "I will show you"[3] (modern-day Israel). In the Old Testament, God promises that Abraham would be known as the

---

[1] Hebrews 8:13
[2] The first five books of the Old Testament are also known as the Pentateuch.
[3] Genesis 12:1

"father of many nations."[4] The Old Testament also introduces us to Abraham's two sons, Ishmael and Isaac. It speaks of Isaac's son, Jacob, and tells why God changed his name to Israel and of the dozen sons he fathered.

The Torah also contains the story of Moses. This man was raised as an adopted son in Pharaoh's household and led his blood relatives, the children of Israel, out of Egypt after their 400-year visit there had soured. However, Moses is best known for having mediated a covenant between God and the Israelites and for bringing the Ten Commandments down from Mount Sinai.

The Old Testament records God's promise of a Messiah, the anointed One, who would come to deliver the Israelites from their oppressors. It also tells how the Israelites, through disobedience to God's commandments, broke the covenant He made with them. And it records God's promise to give them a New Covenant to replace the one they had broken.

The story of God giving the covenant to Moses was of particular interest to me because of my desire to better understand the differences between the *old* and the *new*.

When Moses led Israel's descendants out of Egypt, their journey became known as the Exodus. Their travels took them through the Red Sea and into an inhospitable wilderness that became their temporary home for forty years. It was in that desert, on Mount Sinai, that God made a covenant with the children of Israel. He gave Moses the Ten Commandments and all the rules that would govern their relationship with Him, their interactions with one another and the finer points of daily living. The Scriptures tell of this significant event:

---

[4] Genesis 17:4

In the third month after the Israelites left Egypt . . . they entered the Desert of Sinai, and Israel camped there in the desert in front of the mountain. Then Moses went up to God, and the LORD called to him from the mountain and said, ". . . Now if you *obey me fully and keep my covenant*, then out of all nations you will be my treasured possession. Although the whole earth is mine, you will be for me a kingdom of priests and a holy nation."[5]

After hearing these words, Moses came down from the mountain and brought this good news to the people:

The people all responded together, "We will do everything the LORD has said." So Moses brought their answer back to the LORD.[6]

The Scriptures go on to describe what was happening on the mountain as this interchange between God and Moses unfolded:

Mount Sinai was covered with smoke, because the LORD descended on it in fire. The smoke billowed up from it like smoke from a furnace, the whole mountain trembled violently, and the sound of the trumpet grew louder and louder.[7]

God sent Moses back down to the people with instructions warning them not to approach the mountain under penalty of death. Even an animal that strayed into the forbidden zone was to be killed.

The Israelite people were waiting at the foot of the mountain for Moses to return. The Scriptures record their state of mind:

---

[5] Exodus 19:1-6
[6] Exodus 19:8
[7] Exodus 19:18-19

When the people saw the thunder and lightning and heard the trumpet and saw the mountain in smoke, they trembled with *fear*. They stayed at a distance and said to Moses, "Speak to us yourself and we will listen. But do not have God speak to us or we will die."[8]

Moses tried to reassure them with these words:

Do not be afraid. God has come to test you, so that the *fear* of God will be with you to keep you from sinning.[9]

How effective is fear in keeping us from sinning? There is a saying, "People run best scared." Although that might be true in a short run, it is not the case for a real race. Real races are won by people who love to run, improve on their best time, hear the cheers of the fans and hold trophies in their hands. It's hard to scare someone into winning a real race.

So it was with the Hebrew people. God gave the Ten Commandments to Moses. He brought them down from the mountain and taught them to the people. Their love for God was to be expressed through obedience to His commands. Disobedience to those commands was sin and considered hatred toward God.

The Israelites lived in a black-and-white world. There was a long list of sins that had the death penalty written after them, sins quite a few of us have already committed. Sins that were premeditated or done in anger or arrogance were treated by God with special severity.[10]

All of the people had given their word to Moses saying, "We will do everything the LORD has said." But that was as they stood at

---

[8] Exodus 20:18-19
[9] Exodus 20:20
[10] See Exodus 21:12-14

the base of a trembling mountain covered in smoke with the fear of the Lord upon them. When they were faced with actually keeping the Law with its Ten Commandments, it was harder than they had ever imagined. Some of their best and brightest failed miserably.

Take King David, for example. David, the shepherd boy who became king of Israel, was one of those whose failure was particularly notable. The Scriptures make no secret of the fact that David committed one of the most shocking crimes of all the kings of Israel. He murdered a man in an attempt to cover up an affair he had with the man's wife. The plot to murder the husband became necessary when the woman discovered she was pregnant because of their adulterous relationship.

It would appear that the whole thing started innocently enough one spring evening when David couldn't sleep and went out on the rooftop patio of his palace to get some fresh air. It just so happened that his attention was drawn to a woman who lived in the neighborhood and was taking her post-menstrual purification bath as required by the Law. She was strikingly beautiful.

David sent one of his underlings to find out who she was. Her name was Bathsheba. She was the wife of one of his military men, Uriah. He was away fighting a war for King David.

As the old saying goes, "One thing led to another." Before it was over, David had coveted his neighbor's wife, stolen Bathsheba's affection from her husband and committed adultery with her. When she told David that she was pregnant by him, David lied to her husband—one of his most loyal and devoted soldiers. He told Uriah that he had called him back from the battlefield for some rest and recreation. In actuality, David's plan was that this brief interlude between Uriah and Bathsheba would provide a logical explanation for the child who would be born months later.

However, out of loyalty to his fellow soldiers, Uriah would not sleep with his wife. When King David realized that his plan had failed, he sent Uriah back to the battlefront carrying his own death warrant. The letter Uriah carried contained sealed instructions from the king to the commander of the army ordering that Uriah be killed in battle. Yes, David murdered this loyal soldier in order to cover his own sin of adultery.

If I'm counting right, David broke five of the Ten Commandments. He *coveted* his neighbor's wife, *stole* her affection, *committed adultery*, *lied* to her husband and then *murdered* him. And two of those sins carried a mandatory death penalty.

1. If a man commits adultery with another man's wife—with the wife of his neighbor—both the adulterer and the adulteress must be put to death.[11]

2. If anyone takes the life of a human being, he must be put to death.[12]

But David didn't end up getting the death penalty. Instead, he married Bathsheba.[13] As with most legal systems, there were safeguards and loopholes. "One witness is not enough to convict a man accused of any crime or offense he may have committed. A matter must be established by the testimony of two or three wit-nessses."[14] It seems that no one had actually *seen* David commit adultery or murder.

Be that as it may, no one would accuse King David of being insincere, a phony, a fraud or a God-hater. Quite the contrary, God

---

[11] Leviticus 20:10
[12] Leviticus 24:17
[13] 2 Samuel 11:27
[14] Deuteronomy 19:15

describes David as "a man after his own heart."[15] Yet the truth is that David failed miserably at keeping the Law. Under the terms of the Old Covenant, he deserved to die as a penalty for his sins.

What I realized was this: The Law with its Ten Commandments and *the fear of a death sentence* weren't enough to keep even good people from sinning. God's rules were being broken again and again.

Neither the people of that day nor those of us living presently should be surprised that God announced the coming of a New Covenant. God said that the reason for the New Covenant was that the covenant He had made with the children of Israel at Mount Sinai had been broken. It was broken by the people's failure to do what they had promised—to obey the commands it contained.

Something had to change. Through His prophets, God had begun to prepare the Israelites for the dramatic change that was coming. Here are the words God spoke through Isaiah, one of Israel's prophets, about 700 B.C.:

Forget the former things; do not dwell on the past. See, I am doing a *new thing!*[16]

"Thing" is a word we use when we are being vague about "something." I think this is what God was doing by using the word "thing." He wasn't ready to give them specifics, but they did need to be prepared for the large change that was coming.

One hundred years after these words from Isaiah, God told them what this "new thing" would actually be. It was about 600 B.C. when God made this startling announcement through another of His prophets, Jeremiah:

---

[15] See 1 Samuel 13:14
[16] Isaiah 43:18-19

"The time is coming," declares the LORD, "when I will make a *new covenant* with the house of Israel and with the house of Judah."[17]

The mysterious "new thing" Isaiah had foretold was no longer a mystery. A "New Covenant" was coming! Every person of Hebrew descent should have sat bolt upright when they heard these words. *Covenant* was everything to them. *Covenant* defined how God related to them and how they were to relate to God. It was a binding legal agreement between God and His people.

This announcement came during a time of significant turmoil. They were a divided people: the "house of Israel"—ten of the twelve tribes living in the northern section of the land; and the "house of Judah"—the remaining two tribes living in the southern lands around Jerusalem. Furthermore, most of the Israelite people weren't even residing in their beloved Promised Land. The armies of Assyria and Babylon had forcibly removed them. Only the poorest of them remained in Jerusalem and the tribal territories that had been their home.

The announcement of a coming New Covenant was the kind of news that should have been emblazoned in two-inch headlines on the front page of the *Jerusalem Daily* and the *Babylon Underground Review*: **GOD ANNOUNCES COMING NEW COVENANT.**

The fact that God would make a New Covenant with them was very significant. It would bring profound change for all of Israel, redefining the rules by which they lived and worshiped God.

It was clear from the words "the time is coming" that this was something that would happen at some point in the future. God was giving them advance notice. One thing was certain as they read the

---

[17] Jeremiah 31:31

fine print: This covenant would be *different* from the existing one.

If I were going to understand the significance of the New Covenant, I needed to explore these differences more fully.

CHAPTER 10

Not Like The Covenant

Although I hadn't noticed it before, my attention was now gripped by a phrase spoken by Jeremiah, "It will not be like the covenant."[1] I had never really noticed how important this point was to God. When God announced the coming of a new covenant this was the first thing He wanted Jeremiah to make clear to the people.

> "*It will not be like the covenant* I made with their forefathers when I took them by the hand to lead them out of Egypt, because they broke my covenant, . . ." declares the LORD.[2]

The phrase "not be like" contains words of differentiation, used to highlight the difference between the existing covenant and the one being announced. This was big—very big! There would be significant changes in the New Covenant that was now promised.

As I thought about this, I recognized that it wouldn't have made sense for God to do the same thing over again in light of the fact that the people had failed in their attempt to keep the existing covenant. They had broken that covenant by not doing what they had said. They failed to do what they had promised when they

---

[1] Jeremiah 31:32a
[2] Jeremiah 31:32

stood at the foot of a trembling mountain years earlier saying, "We will do everything the LORD has said."[3]

Now they needed to be prepared for a complete shift—a systemic change—in the way they related to God and in the way He related to them. In fact, Jeremiah had already given them one of the specific ways that the New Covenant would differ from the existing one. It is found in the two sentences just before he announced the coming of a new covenant:

> In those days people will no longer say, "The fathers have eaten sour grapes, and the children's teeth are set on edge." Instead, everyone will die for his own sin; whoever eats sour grapes—his own teeth will be set on edge. The time is coming . . . when I will make a *new covenant.*[4]

It seems that this saying, "The fathers have eaten sour grapes, and the children's teeth are set on edge," was quite popular among the people of Israel at that time. It was the way they expressed how the *faux pas*, moral deficiencies and maladaptive behaviors (sins) of one generation, penalized the next. The children's misaligned teeth were a direct result of God's judgment for sins they had never committed—the sins of their fathers.

Although that may seem unfair, there was good reason for them to attribute the misaligned teeth of the children to the ill effects of the preceding generation's sin. It was part of the covenant God had made with them at Mount Sinai. The second commandment read:

> You shall not make for yourself an idol . . . for I, the LORD your God, am a jealous God, *punishing the children for the sin of the fathers to the third and fourth generation.*[5]

---

[3] Exodus 19:8
[4] Jeremiah 31:29-31
[5] Exodus 20:4-5

There it was in black and white—actually in stone. Under the existing covenant, the failure to love God by obeying His commands had dire consequences on the next three or four generations. The succeeding generations were punished for sins they had never committed. This was the rule mandated by God in the Ten Commandments given to Moses.

The thought of their own children suffering as a consequence of the parent's sin was one more deterrent against breaking God's Law. It made the fence between them and their sinful behavior even more sharply barbed. Nevertheless, no promised punishment was large enough to prevent disobedience.

It is no wonder that David, in writing the Psalms, makes this appeal to God regarding the sins of previous generations:

> Do not hold against us the sins of the fathers; may your mercy come quickly to meet us, for we are in desperate need.[6]

Thankfully, the coming *new covenant* as announced by Jeremiah would *not be like* the covenant God had made with their forefathers. This popular saying about "sour grapes" and "teeth set on edge" would no longer be relevant when this promised New Covenant came. Jeremiah continued:

> Instead, everyone will die for his own sin; whoever eats sour grapes—his own teeth will be set on edge.[7]

One of the prominent characteristics of the promised New Covenant was that each individual would bear the consequences of his own sin. The emphasis would be on personal responsibility and

---

[6] Psalm 79:8
[7] Jeremiah 31:30

accountability.

But this was only one of the ways that the New Covenant would *not be like* the existing covenant. There was more fine print describing the features of the promised New Covenant.

I will put my law in their minds and write it on their hearts.[8]

God was saying that He would personally give His law to each participant in the coming covenant. He would make it a part of their understanding by putting it in their minds and by writing it in the very core of their being—on their hearts.

This represented a dramatic change in the way God would communicate His laws to the people. Hundreds of years earlier, when God had given His commandments to Moses on Mount Sinai, He had written the ten most important points in stone and given them to Moses to teach to the people. Here are the actual words describing what happened:

When the LORD finished speaking to Moses on Mount Sinai, he gave him the two tablets of the Testimony, the tablets of stone *inscribed by the finger of God.*[9]

But in the promised New Covenant, Jeremiah is saying that God would actually write His law on their hearts, not on stone tablets.

In the existing covenant, Moses was the one person who had contact with God. He then passed His words on to the rest of the people. The people wanted it this way. Moses was a go-between.

However, that would change when the New Covenant was enacted. Not only would there be a new level of personal account-

---

[8] Jeremiah 31:33
[9] Exodus 31:18

ability, but there also would be a new level of personal relationship between God and each of His people. Jeremiah's next words seem to confirm this:

I will be their God, and they will be my people.[10]

In this New Covenant, there would be a sense of mutual ownership. God would see them even more personally as *My* people, and the people would view their Creator as *my* God.

And it got even better than that. Jeremiah continued to speak for God:

No longer will a man teach his neighbor, or a man his brother, saying, "Know the LORD," because they will all know me.[11]

It is important to remember that this promise was being made to a communal people. This large ethnic nation was made up of the descendants of the twelve sons of Israel. They lived in family tribes. Unlike the communities that most of us live in today, their neighbors were their relatives, people who believed in the same God and lived under the same covenant.

When God said "no longer will a man teach his neighbor, or . . . his brother," He was not talking about a future in which everyone in the world would know the Lord. Rather, He was talking about a covenant community in which all would know the Lord personally.

That "they will all know me" should not be considered a small improvement promised as part of the "new thing." It was a dramatic change, because under the Old Covenant knowing God was not a common experience. Even the priests and prophets struggled

---

[10] Jeremiah 31:33
[11] Jeremiah 31:34a

in their quest to know Him.[12] But this New Covenant promised to take them to a deeper level of personal intimacy with God. There was more. Jeremiah continued:

> They will *all* know me, from the least of them to the greatest.[13]

All of His people in the New Covenant would enjoy this promised personal intimacy with God. It would transcend age, gender, ethnicity, education, social status and even spiritual office. God was saying that in the coming covenant "They will *all* know me," and that included "the least of them to the greatest."

There was one final advantage to this New Covenant promised through Jeremiah.

> For I will forgive their wickedness and will remember their sins no more.[14]

Under the existing covenant given to Moses, there was a rigorous system of penalties and sacrifices for sin. The sacrifices usually consisted of some kind of animal being killed or symbolically banished by being sent out alone into the wilderness to die. The penalties for breaking one of the commands God had given them ranged from ceremonial to severe. This included a death sentence for a number of sins that are quite common to us today. The promise of the New Covenant that God would "forgive their wickedness" and "remember their sins no more" was an incredible change and a huge benefit.

From even the small amount of information recorded in Jeremiah, it would seem that all would have eagerly anticipated the

---

[12] See 1 Samuel 3:7; Jeremiah 2:8, 4:22

[13] Jeremiah 31:34b

[14] Jeremiah 31:34c

New Covenant. But no one knew how long it would actually be before this promised covenant would be enacted. Nor did they know through whom it would come.

After Jeremiah, the phrase "new covenant" was not recorded again in the Old Testament Scriptures. It would be 600 years before the words "new covenant" would be heard once more and recorded for us to see. And just to make sure the people of Israel were ready to receive this New Covenant, God made it clear that they'd better be listening when the One He sent gave it to them.

That's next.

CHAPTER 11

LISTEN TO HIM!

"They're not listening to me!" I had talked to them a number of times about the temperature in the coffee shop that I now considered my Southern California office. It was freezing—more like cold storage than a coffee shop. In fact, it seemed colder now than when I had been there the year before.

In spite of a mist that was in the early morning air, I had felt comfortable wearing a short-sleeve T-shirt as I walked toward the coffee shop to continue my writing. I had been the first person at the counter when they unlocked the doors at 5:30 a.m.

But immediately, I felt the cold air blowing out of the vents. I found a corner table that was somewhat sheltered and sat down. I had already ordered my oatmeal, but I approached the counter again.

"I'm freezing in here. Is there any way you can turn off the air conditioner?"

A young woman behind the counter assured me that there was nothing that could be done about the temperature, and a young man working the specialty drinks chimed in to affirm the same.

I was scheduled to meet my son-in-law in an hour and a half, so I decided to stay put. It was just after 7:00 a.m. when he slid into the chair opposite me. He was shaking his head from side to side as he mumbled, "I knew there would be a confrontation!"

"What are you talking about?"

"I told them it was freezing in here and asked if they could make it warmer," he answered. "They said no so I told them I had to see the manager. I've been talking to them about this for three years. Look at all the empty seats in this place!"

It was true. The few people who had come in the last hour and a half had left almost immediately.

Just minutes later we saw the manager walking around the near-empty room holding a portable thermometer high in the air.

"Sixty-five degrees!" he exclaimed.

My son-in-law and I high-fived each other. Someone had finally listened to us. And when we left an hour and a half later, it was already considerably warmer. The manager had finally listened and reset the thermostat.

Why was that so difficult? Why do we have such a hard time actually hearing what is being said to us?

The fact is, it's easy to miss some very significant messages that are being spoken to us by customers, wives, husbands, children and God. I didn't have to look any farther than myself to see it. I hadn't heard the One·Command that Jesus had given.

I think God knows that listening is not one of our strong points as human beings. I believe this was demonstrated when Jesus took three of His disciples—Peter, James and John—up onto a high mountain. That day they saw Jesus as they had never seen Him before.

There he was transfigured before them. His face shone like

the sun, and his clothes became as white as the light.[1]

What happened next only added to the wonder of what they were witnessing.

Just then there appeared before them Moses and Elijah, talking with Jesus.[2]

Peter, seldom at a loss for words, seized the moment by making the following declaration:

Lord, it is good for us to be here. If you wish, I will put up three shelters—one for you, one for Moses and one for Elijah.[3]

But as he was speaking, Peter was interrupted by a voice that spoke from a bright cloud that enveloped them:

This is my Son, whom I love; with him I am well pleased. *Listen to him!*[4]

"Listen to Him!" God was now making His point very clear—in a most dramatic fashion. It was a point they could not afford to miss.

When they looked up, they saw no one except Jesus.[5]

Moses and Elijah were no longer part of the scene. They had already spoken the words God had given them to speak. Now God wanted His people to listen to His Son.

"Listen to Him!" Another thing that I hadn't noticed before was

---

[1] Matthew 17:2
[2] Matthew 17:3
[3] Matthew 17:4
[4] Matthew 17:5
[5] Matthew 17:8

that these were the exact words that had been spoken by God to Moses more than 1,300 years earlier in reference to Jesus' coming. It happened when the Israelites were gathered at Mount Sinai in the wilderness. God was giving them the Ten Commandments.

> When the people saw the thunder and lightning and heard the trumpet and saw the mountain in smoke, they trembled with fear. They stayed at a distance and said to Moses, "Speak to us yourself and we will listen. But do not have God speak to us or we will die."[6]

The Scripture records God's words to Moses for the people:

> The LORD said to me: "What they say is good. I will raise up for them a prophet like you from among their brothers; I will put my words in his mouth, and he will tell them everything I command him. If anyone does *not listen* to my words that the prophet speaks in my name, I myself will call him to account."[7]

When Moses delivered God's message to the people at the foot of the mountain, he put it in these prophetic words:

> The LORD your God will raise up for you a prophet like me from among your own brothers. *You must listen to him.*[8]

Now 1,300 years later, God was delivering the same message to Peter, James and John on this Mount of Transfiguration. The cameo appearance of Moses and Elijah was intentional and telling. Their presence brought to mind the prophecies concerning the Prophet who was to come.

The Law, as represented by Moses, and the Prophets, as repre-

---

[6] Exodus 20:18-19
[7] Deuteronomy 18:17-19
[8] Deuteronomy 18:15

sented by Elijah, were now finding their fulfillment in the One they had foretold. The Prophet was Jesus, and He was here. The giver of the promised New Covenant had come. The Law of Christ would now fulfill the Law of Moses. But we had to *listen to Him!*

For me, all of this came in the context of having missed some very important words that Jesus had spoken. Although I had embraced the New Covenant, I had missed the New Commandment, the one He owned as "My Command"! It was as if I had failed to *listen to Jesus.*

So many Scriptures pointed to Jesus' coming and to His ultimate place of importance. Yet in my own thinking and practice, it seems as if I had put Jesus' words on an equal plane with all the other words of inspired Scripture. I had really not given His words the place of supremacy they were intended to have. He was much more than a speaker of God-breathed words. He was the Word made flesh. He was God's Message—literally walking among us.

John the apostle said it in this way:

In the beginning was the Word, and the Word was with God, and the Word was God.[9]

The Word became flesh and made his dwelling among us. We have seen his glory, the glory of the One and Only, who came from the Father, full of grace and truth.[10]

The writer of Hebrews gives us this perspective on the uniqueness and importance of the message Jesus was:

In the past God spoke to our forefathers through the prophets at many times and in various ways, but in these

---

[9] John 1:1
[10] John 1:14

last days he has spoken to us by his Son, whom he appointed heir of all things, and through whom he made the universe. The Son is the radiance of God's glory and the exact representation of his being.[11]

Why is it so imperative that we listen to Jesus? Because God said that He would hold accountable those who did not listen to the words of the One to come. Jesus said this of the words He spoke:

> As for the person who hears my words but does not keep them, I do not judge him. For I did not come to judge the world, but to save it. There is a judge for the one who rejects me and does not accept my words; that very word which I spoke will condemn him at the last day. For I did not speak of my own accord, but the Father who sent me commanded me what to say and how to say it. I know that his command leads to eternal life. So whatever I say is just what the Father has told me to say.[12]

We must *listen to Him!* And that certainly includes the New Command He gave, the One Command He owned as "My Command."

Jesus spoke this New Command on His last night with the disciples before His crucifixion. He and His handpicked Twelve were gathered in an upper room in Jerusalem to celebrate the historic Passover meal. Now I was realizing that Jesus had introduced both the New Command and the New Covenant on that special night.

I needed to explore the relationship between these two.

---

[11] Hebrews 1:1-3
[12] John 12:47-50

CHAPTER 12

NEW COVENANT,
NEW COMMANDMENT

For the first time, I was confronting the fact that Jesus announced the New Covenant and the New Commandment on the same night. Was this merely coincidental, or did Jesus intend for the New Covenant and the New Commandment to be linked?

Now I had to know if Jesus intended for them to be connected. If so, the importance of His Command was even more significant and the loss of the Command of even greater consequence than I had thought. I needed to take a closer look at how both were introduced.

Possibly the most important truths that Jesus ever gave His disciples are found in the words He spoke to them on the eve of His crucifixion. Here is how I envision that pivotal night unfolding.

The Feast of Unleavened Bread had come, and Jesus' disciples asked Him where they should have the Passover meal. Jesus said:

> Go into the city to a certain man and tell him, "The Teacher says: My appointed time is near. I am going to celebrate the Passover with my disciples at your house." So the disciples did as Jesus had directed them and prepared the Passover.[1]

---

[1] Matthew 26:18-19

When Passover evening arrived, "Jesus was reclining at the table with the Twelve."[2] As they were eating, Jesus "took bread, gave thanks and broke it, and gave it to them, saying, 'This is my body given for you; do this in remembrance of me.' "[3] Then He took the cup in His hand and made this proclamation:

> This cup is the *new covenant* in my blood, which is poured out for you.[4]

Jeremiah's promise, "the time is coming," had *now come!* The promised *New Covenant* would be enacted. Six hundred years of scriptural silence concerning the coming New Covenant was broken as Jesus spoke those words.

After they had eaten the meal, Jesus then "showed them the full extent of his love."[5] He took off His street clothes, wrapped Himself in a towel and washed His disciples' feet. When Jesus had finished, He told them that He had just given them a model of servant leadership they should follow.[6]

Next, He broke the startling news that one of them would turn on Him in an act of betrayal. It was only moments later that Judas hurriedly left the room. Some thought he went to buy more food for the feast; others assumed that he had gone to give urgently needed money to an impoverished citizen. After all, Judas was the treasurer for Jesus and His company of disciples.

The events of the evening were now moving at a rapid pace. The promise of thirty pieces of silver was propelling Judas through the streets of Jerusalem toward those who had for months been seeking

---

[2] Matthew 26:20
[3] Luke 22:19
[4] Luke 22:20
[5] John 13:1
[6] See John 13:15-17

a way to arrest Jesus.

Jesus continued speaking to the eleven who remained. He explained that He would be leaving them, and they could not go with Him on this journey. Having just announced the New Covenant in His blood, He now announced the New Command:

> A *new command* I give you: Love one another. As I have loved you, so you must love one another. By this all men will know that you are my disciples, if you love one another.[7]

Their obedience to this New Command, based on His love for them, would forever be their mark of authenticity. By this people everywhere would identify them as His disciples—Christians, in the modern vernacular.

Jesus repeated the New Command two more times before that night was over, only now He owned it as "My Command."

> *My command* is this: Love each other as I have loved you.[8]

> This is *my command:* Love each other.[9]

The promised *New Covenant* was now being enacted; the *New Commandment* had been given.

In the past, this connection had never been clear to me. But now I saw the unmistakable link—one central to authentic Christianity. *The New Covenant came with the New Command.* The two are intertwined.

The covenant God made at Mount Sinai is linked with the Ten Commandments He gave through Moses. The New Covenant God

---

[7] John 13:34-35
[8] John 15:12
[9] John 15:17

made in Jerusalem is linked with the One Commandment Jesus gave on the eve of His crucifixion. The New Covenant and the New Command are inextricably linked.

Astonishingly, through decades of Christian ministry and teaching, the New Covenant and the New Commandment had never been connected in my own thinking and theology. But now that connection seemed undeniable to me. Jesus had intentionally linked the New Covenant and the New Commandment by introducing both of them on this pivotal night! The New Commandment and the New Covenant were as inseparable as the Ten Commandments and the covenant God had made with the Israelites at Mount Sinai.

As a Christian, I had readily embraced the following *new* elements of the New Covenant:

NEW COVENANT

> He took the cup, saying, "This cup is the *new covenant* in my blood, which is poured out for you."[10]

NEW BIRTH

> Praise be to the God and Father of our Lord Jesus Christ! In his great mercy he has given us *new birth* into a living hope through the resurrection of Jesus Christ from the dead.[11]

NEW CREATION

> Therefore, if anyone is in Christ, he is a *new creation;* the old has gone, the new has come![12]

---

[10] Luke 22:20
[11] 1 Peter 1:3
[12] 2 Corinthians 5:17

> Neither circumcision nor uncircumcision means anything; what counts is a *new creation*.[13]

NEW LIFE

> We were therefore buried with him through baptism into death in order that, just as Christ was raised from the dead through the glory of the Father, we too may live a *new life*.[14]

NEW MAN

> His purpose was to create in himself one *new man* out of the two, thus making peace, and in this one body to reconcile both of them to God through the cross, by which he put to death their hostility.[15]

NEW SELF

> Put on the *new self*, created to be like God in true righteousness and holiness.[16]

NEW WAY OF THE SPIRIT

> But now, by dying to what once bound us, we have been released from the law so that we serve in the *new way of the Spirit*, and not in the old way of the written code.[17]

As a part of my journey of discovery, I had to add to my list the *New Command* Jesus had given us. It was the one commandment He owned as "My Command" and the one He identified as the mark of authenticity for those who would follow Him!

---

[13] Galatians 6:15
[14] Romans 6:4
[15] Ephesians 2:15-16
[16] Ephesians 4:24
[17] Romans 7:6

NEW COMMAND

A *new command* I give you: Love one another. As I have loved you, so you must love one another. By this all men will know that you are my disciples, if you love one another.[18]

Without realizing it, I had been embracing the New Covenant but then awkwardly linking it with the commandments that were given with the Old Covenant. In so doing, I'd been attempting to live in two covenants at once—something impossible to do. I'd been living in what I've since come to think of as a "no-man's land" between the two covenants. In that position I was vulnerable to confusion and condemnation, having missed the empowerment that comes through the simplicity of the *new*.

The Ten Commandments given by Moses were written in stone and carried in the Ark of the Covenant—God's dwelling place in that day. The One Commandment given by Jesus is now written on the hearts of those who believe in Him and is carried inside of them; God's dwelling place today is inside of us.

As Jeremiah had promised long ago, in this New Covenant God has not only written the Law on our hearts, He has put that Law in our minds as well.

"This is the covenant . . .," declares the LORD. "I will put my law in their minds and write it on their hearts. I will be their God, and they will be my people. No longer will a man teach his neighbor, or a man his brother . . ."[19]

Isaiah, too, had foretold this when he wrote, "All your sons will

---

[18] John 13:34-35
[19] Jeremiah 31:33-34

be taught by the LORD, and great will be your children's peace."[20] Jesus had quoted these words in His teaching when He said, "It is written in the Prophets: 'They will all be taught by God.' Everyone who listens to the Father and learns from him comes to me."[21]

As I searched the Scriptures, I found only one other place that seemed to match these prophetic declarations. It was written 700 years after Isaiah had first said, "All your sons will be taught by the LORD." I discovered it in Paul's first letter to the Christians in Thessalonica. He wrote, "You yourselves have been taught by God."

What lesson was so important to God that He would *personally* teach it—put it in their minds—and *personally* inscribe it—write it on their hearts? Paul tells us what that lesson was:

Now about brotherly love we do not need to write to you, for you yourselves have been *taught by God to love each other.*[22]

I was astonished to see what I had never comprehended before. Jesus' Command was the lesson God personally taught and inscribed on their hearts: *Love each other!* This is what the prophets had foretold.

The promised New Covenant had been given, and God was now teaching the New Commandment. This time, however, He was writing it "not with ink but with the Spirit of the living God, not on tablets of stone but on tablets of human hearts."[23]

And God wanted to do all that He offered under the New Covenant, not only for the Israelite nation, but for all peoples—Jews

---

[20] Isaiah 54:13
[21] John 6:45
[22] 1 Thessalonians 4:9
[23] 2 Corinthians 3:3

and Gentiles alike.

It was this part of the New Covenant that next captured my attention.

CHAPTER 13

ONE NEW PERSON

I could now see more clearly than ever the "new" that was emerging out of the "old." The New Covenant that God promised to Israel was to be fully embraced by the Hebrew people. It was their New Covenant. It fulfilled the words that had been spoken in their Torah and by their prophets. Far from replacing the Jews, the New Covenant opened the door by which they would fulfill their divine destiny, broadening their strategic role as a chosen people.

However, the New Covenant was not for the Jews alone; they were to share it. Other nations, those known as Gentiles, were now invited to join them. Jews and Gentiles would be united as one family of faith—all children of the heavenly Father. A "new person" was being created; a new unity was being forged. Through Jesus, the promised Messiah, God's "purpose was to create . . . one new man out of the two."[1]

This inclusion of the Gentiles was part of the "new thing" that had been promised by the prophets. King David was one of those who had foretold of this "new thing" in his poetic and prophetic Psalms. He said that Israel's song of worship—the solo they had sung—would someday become a chorus, the voices of the

---

[1] Ephesians 2:15

nations! In this expanded role, Israel would lead the nations in singing a "new song."

> Sing to the LORD a new song; sing to the LORD, all the earth. Sing to the LORD, praise his name; proclaim his salvation day after day. Declare his glory among the nations, his marvelous deeds among all peoples. . . . Ascribe to the LORD, O families of nations, ascribe to the LORD glory and strength. . . . Say among the nations, "The LORD reigns."[2]

The word "nations" referred to the Gentile ethnicities, people who had previously worshiped idols made with their own hands. With the advent of the New Covenant, these nations were invited to join those who had formerly lived under the covenant given by God through Moses.

Jesus spoke of this enlarged company of covenant people to those Jews who followed Him.

> I am the good shepherd; I know my sheep and my sheep know me . . . and I lay down my life for the sheep. I have other sheep that are not of this sheep pen. I must bring them also. They too will listen to my voice, and there shall be one flock and one shepherd.[3]

The two—Jews and Gentiles—would become "one flock" with "one shepherd." Paul, with his first-hand knowledge of Jewish history, explains this amazing change and God's plan to join the two ethnicities into one new person.

> Therefore, remember that formerly you who are Gentiles by birth . . . were separate from Christ, excluded from

---

2 Psalm 96:1-3, 7, 10
3 John 10:14-16

citizenship in Israel and foreigners to the covenants of the promise, without hope and without God in the world. But now in Christ Jesus you who once were far away have been brought near through the blood of Christ. For he himself is our peace, who has made the two one and has destroyed the barrier, the dividing wall of hostility, by abolishing in his flesh the law with its commandments and regulations.[4]

Then Paul goes on to explain why God had done it this way and the outcomes that He desired:

His purpose was to create in himself one new man out of the two, thus making peace, and in this one body to reconcile both of them to God through the cross, by which he put to death their hostility. He came and preached peace to you who were far away and peace to those who were near. For through him we both have access to the Father by one Spirit.[5]

In order to make this abundantly clear to the early Gentile believers, Paul continues by telling them how this had altered their standing in God's family:

Consequently, you are no longer foreigners and aliens, but fellow citizens with God's people and members of God's household, built on the foundation of the apostles and prophets, with Christ Jesus himself as the chief corner-stone. In him the whole building is joined together and rises to become a holy temple in the Lord. And in him you too are being built together to become a dwelling in which God lives by his Spirit.[6]

---

[4] Ephesians 2:11-15a
[5] Ephesians 2:15b-18
[6] Ephesians 2:19-22

This was a seismic change. Now all who believed the message that Jesus brought would be members of God's household. Paul affirmed this when he said, "I am not ashamed of the gospel, because it is the power of God for the salvation of everyone who believes: first for the Jew, then for the Gentile."[7] Jesus' One Command was an indispensable part of that message. It was imperative that they love one another as Jesus had loved them for the wonders of the New Covenant to be demonstrated!

The Jews, who had formerly lived under the Old Covenant and Law given through Moses, would embrace the New Covenant and the New Commandment. This would require a dramatic transition for those who had experienced life under the "old," but would soon embrace the "new." Those who had lived under the covenant given at Mount Sinai would now release it in order to embrace the New Covenant—one with better promises.[8] The writer of Hebrews describes this transition from the "old" to the "new" in these words:

> By calling this covenant "new," he has made the first one obsolete; and what is obsolete and aging will soon disappear.[9]

This also would be a large change for the Gentiles—those who had lived without God's Law. They could no longer be a lawless people. Gentiles who put their faith in Jesus Christ would now be called to embrace the Law of Christ and the New Command.

Together, Jews and Gentiles would live in the New Covenant. They would (1) put their faith in Jesus the Messiah, "the Lamb of God, who takes away the sin of the world!"[10] And they would (2)

---

[7] Romans 1:16
[8] Hebrews 8:6
[9] Hebrews 8:13
[10] John 1:29

follow Jesus' Command—"Love each other as I have loved you."[11]

Paul understood this and gave us a strong mandate in these words:

> I urge you to live a life worthy of the calling you have received. Be completely humble and gentle; be patient, bearing with one another in love. Make every effort to keep the unity of the Spirit through the bond of peace. There is one body and one Spirit—just as you were called to one hope when you were called—one Lord, one faith, one baptism; one God and Father of all, who is over all and through all and in all.[12]

Unity is a gift that God had given His church by the Spirit. It was never designed to be maintained without obedience to Jesus' Command—a resilient love for one another!

As I contemplated this new thought, I began to see church history in a whole new light. When the early church leaders allowed the New Command to slip out of their sight, they lost far more than they could have imagined. Love for one another was what united them, what knit them together. Without love, fracture was inevitable.

To me it now seemed clear that the division that started in biblical times between Jewish believers in Christ and Gentile believers would only grow in the absence of Jesus' Command. Indeed, cracks would begin to fracture the church by the fifth century. By the eleventh century, the church would divide into Eastern and Western branches. In the sixteenth century, the Western church would further split into Roman Catholic and Protestant segments. The Protestant wing would then go on to splinter into hundreds of

---

[11] John 15:12
[12] Ephesians 4:1-6

pieces—each claiming to have an essential truth that validated its existence.

But I now was seeing a new hope for unity! This unity would come as those who embraced God's New Covenant discovered the New Commandment. For unity to be restored, we will be required to trust deeply in Jesus and obey the Command He has given us.

In this new understanding, my attention was drawn once again to the night that Jesus announced the New Covenant and gave His New Command. After supper that evening, Jesus prayed an impassioned prayer to the Father, a prayer in which He used the word "one" as an expression of unity.

First, Jesus used the word "one" in His prayer for the eleven disciples who remained with Him in that fateful hour.

> Holy Father, protect them by the power of your name—the name you gave me—so that they may be *one* as we are one.[13]

Then, in the following verses, I noticed some things that had never caught my attention before. In those Scriptures, Jesus used the word "one" several more times as He now prayed for those who would believe at a future point in time.

> My prayer is not for them alone. I pray also for those who will believe in me through their message, that all of them may be *one*, Father, just as you are in me and I am in you. May they also be in us so that the world may believe that you have sent me. I have given them the glory that you gave me, that they may be *one* as we are one: I in them and you in me.[14]

---

[13] John 17:11
[14] John 17:20-23a

But Jesus had not yet finished His prayer to the Father for us. He now linked this unity—being one—with the Father's love for each of us as children in His family. Jesus was praying for unity—a unity that would only come about when we began to live out His Command. And that unity would be recognized as a sign that Jesus had been truly sent by God and that His followers were loved by the Father.

> May they be brought to complete unity to let the world know that you sent me and have loved them even as you have loved me.[15]

I was now fully persuaded that unity among His followers was no small matter to Jesus. Neither should it be a small matter to those who are His devoted followers.

Jesus was the Jewish Messiah. The New Covenant belonged to the Jews; it was promised to them by their prophets. As such, they were given a leading role. But they were not to lead others back into their past. They were to lead all of us together into our collective future—a future that would not replace them, but rather fulfill their destiny by drawing in Gentiles also.

The New Covenant and the New Command now belonged to all who believed in Jesus Christ. We are united—one new person!

That was God's plan, but as I've mentioned earlier, I had come face-to-face with my personal loss of Jesus' Command. And I had also been stunned by the loss of His Command by the early church fathers (A.D. 125–325).

That brought me back to another important question: If the

---

[15] John 17:23b

Command Jesus gave us was lost early in church history, had it been discovered again at some point during the past 1,800 years?

CHAPTER 14

LOST AND FOUND?

That question propelled me into long hours of searching church history. This search reinforced the fact that I was not alone in my oversight of this pivotal command. Many of the powerful messages about love in our long Christian history also failed to make a direct connection between Jesus' Command and the many references to love in the New Testament Scriptures.

Augustine of Hippo is a very significant figure in Christian history, in my opinion the most influential in the last 1,600 years. Some have called him "the father of theology." Having both a powerful testimony of conversion and a brilliant mind, he was a prolific writer. His insights into Jesus' Command are recorded in his lecture on John 13:34-35 in the year A.D. 416:

> The Lord Jesus declares that He is giving His disciples . . . a new commandment, that we should love one another, as He also hath loved us. This is the love that renews us, making us new men, heirs of the New Testament, singers of the new song. It was this love, brethren beloved, that renewed . . . the blessed apostles: it is . . . now renewing the nations, and from among the universal race of man . . . is making and gathering together a new people, the body of the newly-married spouse of the only-begotten Son of God . . . renewed . . . by the new commandment.

To me, finding these words represented one of the most hopeful moments in my search. However, this was only point one in Augustine's lecture that day. Then came point two:

> Think not then, my brethren, that when the Lord says, "A new commandment I give unto you, that ye love one another," there is any overlooking *of that greater commandment*, which requires us to love the Lord our God with all our heart, and with all our soul, and with all our mind; for along with this seeming oversight, the words "that ye love one another" appear also as if they had no reference to that second commandment, which says, "Thou shall love thy neighbor as thyself." For "on these two commandments," He says, "hang all the law and the prophets."[1]

Unfortunately, it was point two that would carry the day for Augustine. He repeated this two-part summary of the Law of Moses over twenty times in his writings. In his mind and theology, Jesus' two-part answer to a question about the Law of Moses overshadowed the New Command Jesus owned as "My Commandment."

Although Jesus said that all the Law and Prophets hung on the two commands—to love God and to love our neighbor—it appears that Augustine took the liberty to hang the New Testament on them as well.

> For this love embraces both the love of God and the love of our neighbor, and "on these two commandments hang all the law and the prophets," *we may add the Gospel and the apostles.*[2]

"We may add the Gospel and the apostles?" Personally, I found

---

[1] St. Augustin: "Homilies on the Gospel of John," *The Nicene and Post-Nicene Fathers*, Vol. 7, ed. Philip Schaff (Albany: AGES Digital Library, 1997), 636-637.

[2] St. Augustin: "The Enchiridion," *The Nicene and Post-Nicene Fathers*, Series 1, Vol. 3, ed. Philip Schaff, (Albany: AGES Digital Library, 1997), 542.

it troubling that Augustine made this addition.

It seemed to me that he struggled to give the New Command, the one that Jesus owned as His, its rightful place in New Covenant theology. A hopeful moment of recovery for Jesus' Command was missed. One of the most eminent voices in our long Christian history had spoken with an uncertain sound. And this uncertainty resounded throughout church history.

Next I searched the *Canons and Dogmatic Decrees from the Seven Councils* of the church spanning the fourth through eighth centuries. I found no direct reference to Jesus' Command.

Then I looked to the Reformation period of the 1500s. There were hopeful moments when it looked as if Jesus' Command had been rediscovered and that recovery would soon follow. We are indebted to Martin Luther for translating the New Testament from Latin into contemporary language. He showed profound insights into Jesus' Command as he expounded the Scriptures he had come to treasure.

One of Luther's most lasting legacies was the *Augsburg Confession* (1530). Would it bring a rediscovery of the Command? I searched through this important document and realized it did not. Although Luther had at times taught convincingly on Jesus' Command, the Augsburg Confession focused on the important *first core commandment* of Christian discipleship—faith in Jesus Christ. It contained more than one hundred references to *faith, belief* or *trust* in God, but mentioned *love* only three times and *charity* only three times. And none of these uses were in direct reference to the Command Jesus gave us.

In general, Luther's Augsburg Confession became the doctrinal foundation for the Lutheran Church, the Anglican Church, the Methodist Church, the holiness movement and the Pentecostal movement. To their credit, these groups inherited the emphasis on faith contained in the Augsburg Confession. But they also inherited the absence of the important *second core commandment*—Jesus' Command that we love one another as He had loved us.

Of all the branches of the Reformation, the Anabaptists[3], who began forming in Europe after 1520, had the clearest grasp of Jesus' Command. Their teachings were more rooted in Jesus' words as recorded in the Gospels and less influenced by the writings of the early church fathers and theologians who followed.

They started well; however, for some in their ranks, "The Rule of Christ"[4] won out over the Command of Christ. The Rule of Christ was their title for the four-step plan based on Matthew 18:15-17, a plan that culminated in shunning those who violated the tenants of their faith. Over time, this resulted in many divisions among them over speculative doctrines and led to painful wounds among sincere believers.

To their credit, some of the branches of the Mennonites (Anabaptist) still make direct reference to Jesus' Command in their contemporary statement of faith and practice. (As difficult as I found it to believe, direct reference to Jesus' Command is not found in the statements of faith of the majority of Western denominations existing today.)

John Calvin's brilliant mind and outstanding education enabled him to make very profound and hopeful commentary on Jesus' Command. I found his writings on John's Gospel and first letter to be some of the most inspiring of all. Yet he seemed to lack a prac-

---

[3] "A member of any of various Protestant sects . . . that denied the validity of infant baptism, baptized believers only, and advocated social and economic reforms as well as the complete separation of church and state." (*Random House Webster's Unabridged Dictionary*)

[4] Robert Friedmann, *The Theology of Anabaptism*, (Scottdale: Herald Press, 1972), 43.

tical application of this precious truth in his personal life and in the church he oversaw in Geneva. In practice, he also appeared to favor the Law of Moses over the Law of Christ.

One of Calvin's most influential works was *The Institutes of the Christian Religion,* a book he labored over for much of his adult life. First published in 1536, the final edition was released twenty-three years later in 1559. It has been a guiding light for many in the Reformed wing of Protestantism over the past 450 years. Although it is nearly 1,700 pages in length, Calvin makes no direct reference to Jesus' Command within its pages, an omission that reinforced my earlier observation.

It is hard to find a major figure in church history who stressed the importance of Christian love more than John Wesley (1703-1791). As I searched through 11,000 pages of his sermons, journals, letters and commentaries, his passion is very clear. Wesley's favorite verse on loving one another was taken from John the apostle's first letter, "Beloved, if God so loved us, we ought also to love one another."[5]

The importance of loving one another was so woven through the fabric of Wesley's life that I found examples of it even in the grammar lessons he wrote:

A Verb must always be of the same Number and Person with the Noun or Pronoun going before it; as, "I love you." "Christians love one another."[6]

Wesley's true passion is revealed in his commentary on John's words in his first letter, "This is his command: to believe in the name of his Son, Jesus Christ, and to love one another as he

---

[5] 1 John 4:11 KJV

[6] *The Works of John Wesley,* Third Edition, Vol. 14, Grammars, Musical Work, Letters (1872) 18.

commanded us."[7] With regard to this verse, Wesley wrote the following:

> And this is his commandment—All his commandments in one word. That we should believe and love—in the manner and degree which he hath taught. This is the greatest and most important command that ever issued from the throne of glory. If this be neglected, no other can be kept; if this be observed, all others are easy.[8]

In spite of Wesley's passionate pleas for believers to love one another, he lamented the lack of love that he saw in many who professed Christian faith. He longed for a return to the days when observers would again say, "See how they love one another."

Although I found five direct references to Jesus' Command in his writings, Wesley did not cite the New Command as the primary text for any of his 141 sermons that are recorded. Wesley's brief commentary on John 13:34 seems understated, a probable indicator of why he never used it as the primary text in any of the sermons he left us.

Thus, after many months of research, I came to the sad conclusion that I was not alone in my oversight of Jesus' Command. By and large, love has remained only a *subset* of Christian truth and teaching. It has not been given priority as a *core commandment* of authentic Christianity.

In reality, our understanding of all the teachings about *love for one another* that are found in the New Testament letters should naturally flow out of the One Command that Jesus gave us. Although this is built on all that God had communicated in the Old

---

[7] 1 John 3:23

[8] John Wesley, *Notes on the Whole Bible* (Albany: AGES Digital Library, 1997), 832.

Testament, Jesus called it a "new command." It's important that we do not leave the impression that the Christian doctrine about love is primarily ours from the Old Testament *or* from Peter, James, John or Paul. Jesus is the author of Christianity. He made love *His Commandment!* He also established Himself as the standard and model of what *loving one another* is to look like.

With Jesus' One Command as the backdrop, I needed to take a new look at the New Testament. What did the New Testament letters have to say about the Command Jesus gave us?

To answer that question, I would first turn to one of the earliest epistles, the letter written by James to Jewish believers.

CHAPTER 15

THE KING'S LAW

It was now clear to me that there was a strategic connection between the One Command Jesus gave us and the many teachings about love in the rest of the New Testament.

Why didn't I make that connection earlier? I see a number of reasons for this. First, I simply did not see Jesus' Command as a *real commandment*. Rather, I viewed it as one more truth in a series of teachings that Jesus gave to His disciples. I now see that although all truth in the Bible is equally true, not all truth is equally important. When Jesus said, "This is my command," He was assigning it the highest priority among the things He taught us.

Second, I had not made the connection between the New Covenant and the New Command. The fact that Jesus announced them both on the same night had not been clear in my mind or my theology. I did not see them as being inextricably linked.

Third, I did not understand the connection between *covenant* and *commandment* in Hebrew history. That connection was understood and assumed in Judaism. The Ten Commandments given by God to Moses were literally kept inside of the Ark of the Covenant.

There was nothing in the ark except the two stone tablets

that Moses had placed in it at Horeb, where the LORD made a covenant with the Israelites . . .[1]

In fact, the Ten Commandments were the words of the covenant. That is clear from the Torah.

He wrote on the tablets the words of the covenant—the Ten Commandments.[2]

Now I clearly saw that *covenant* and *commandment* were connected. This was taking on new and strategic importance in my thinking.

Fourth, I did not see the Command Jesus gave us as the source—the fountainhead—out of which flowed the vast amount of teaching about *loving one another* in the New Testament. I now see that Jesus, as "the author and finisher of our faith,"[3] would naturally be expected to be the source and initiator of such a central truth in Christian doctrine.

Because the writers of the New Testament knew His Command, their teaching about love was not just another subset of doctrinal truth. Rather, their New Testament letters are like a thick forest of application about how we are to *love one another*. These writings are brimming with insights concerning *what is* and *what is not* loving behavior.

While considering these points, I found myself thinking about how difficult the transition must have been for those first Jewish believers, those who had accepted Jesus as the Messiah. They were stepping out of the familiar—what they had known for centuries— to embrace the *new*. Both the size and significance of this change cannot be overestimated.

---

[1] 1 Kings 8:9
[2] Exodus 34:28
[3] Hebrews 12:2 KJV

In one of His first lessons, Jesus had pointed out how difficult this change would be for the Jewish people. He did it with a story about wine and wineskins.

> And no one pours new wine into old wineskins. If he does, the new wine will burst the skins, the wine will run out and the wineskins will be ruined. No, new wine must be poured into new wineskins. And no one after drinking old wine wants the new, for he says, "The old is better."[4]

Yet those who believed the message that Jesus brought were being asked to choose the *new* over the familiar and well-aged *old*. It was a new season. New wineskins would be filled with a fresh infusion of the Spirit. The Holy Spirit would empower the people of the New Covenant to live in the heavenly culture of a coming Kingdom. Moreover, with the promised New Covenant and New Command, the sacred Old Testament Scriptures would soon be joined by New Testament Scriptures.

Many believe that the first New Testament Scripture written was the letter James sent to "the twelve tribes scattered among the nations."[5] His letter was written decades *before* John's Gospel and letters—those New Testament books that give us the clearest statement of the Command Jesus gave.

James had emerged as the overseer of the church in Jerusalem—the earliest and most Jewish Christian congregation. The members of the Jerusalem congregation had known only the Law of Moses before believing in Jesus as Messiah. James was confronted with the challenge of pastoring the first believers who would be governed by the long-promised, but freshly enacted, New Covenant.

---

[4] Luke 5:37-39
[5] James 1:1

In my thinking, James was at a bit of a disadvantage for the role he had been given. He was known as "James the younger"[6] and was not one of the Twelve Jesus had tutored for three years. In fact, James[7] had not become a believer in Jesus until after His resurrection.[8] As a result, he had to learn the lessons Jesus taught from others.

To me, it also seemed significant to note that James had not been present at the Last Supper when Jesus gave the New Commandment. He hadn't heard Jesus say, "A new command I give you: Love one another. As I have loved you, so you must love one another."[9]

However, James was one of the 120 who had gathered in an upper room after Jesus' ascension. As instructed by Jesus, they were waiting for the promised Holy Spirit who would guide, teach and empower the new believers. No doubt, he had heard the apostles in the room talking about the New Covenant and the Command Jesus had given them at the Last Supper. James would also have experienced the heavenly culture of love for one another that was so clearly demonstrated in the church of Jerusalem in those early years.

It is important to recognize that James had no New Testament Scriptures upon which to rely. There was no written Gospel account or letters with a description of the Command Jesus had given. Yet he knew that there was now a law that fulfilled and superseded the Law of Moses.

---

[6] See Mark 15:40

[7] Jesus had chosen two others named James. One was James, the brother of John the apostle. These brothers were the sons of Zebedee. The other James was the son of Alphaeus.

[8] See Matthew 13:55; Mark 6:3

[9] John 13:34

As James wrote what would become the first New Testament letter, he reached back into the only Scriptures available to him, the Old Testament, and chose one phrase from the book of Leviticus upon which to base the new law that was now governing them. The small phrase he chose seemed rather obscure, found only one time in the Torah. Nevertheless, it was well-known in that day, "Love your neighbor as yourself."[10]

I was well aware that Jesus, in answer to a question, had once cited this as the second most important commandment in the Law of Moses. But now James seized on these words and brought them forward for the first time into the New Covenant and the life of the emerging Christian church.

It is important to note that in doing this James is not attempting to bring the two core commandments of the Old Testament forward into the New. As I mentioned earlier, that two-part summary of the Law was never repeated by any of the New Testament writers.

Rather, James, in the absence of any New Testament writings, used this scriptural quotation—"love your neighbor as yourself"—as the basis for expressing the New Command Jesus had given. But even as James reached back into the Torah for this commandment, he knew that it was different—*new*—fulfilling and exceeding all that had gone before. To distinguish the *new* from the *old*, he gave it a new title, the *royal law*. [11]

If you really keep the *royal law* found in Scripture, "Love your neighbor as yourself," you are doing right.

I believe the words "royal law"—*basilikon nomos*—would have

---

[10] Leviticus 19:18

[11] James 2:8

been better translated "King's Law,"[12] because the Greek word *basilikon* actually means "belonging to a king."[13] In giving it the title "King's Law," James is elevating it to a place that is higher than the Law of Moses. Moses was not a king, but now the kingdom of heaven was coming, and the King had given His Command. It would be the law of the land for all of those in His domain.

In writing his letter, James already has laid the foundation for the King's Law. Earlier in his letter, he refers to this new law as "the perfect law that gives freedom."

> But the man who looks intently into *the perfect law that gives freedom,* and continues to do this, not forgetting what he has heard, but doing it—he will be blessed in what he does.[14]

For James, this perfect law was expressed as the King's Law, *loving your neighbor as yourself.*

Because most of us live in a secular society, we assume that the word "neighbor" used here referred to someone like the people living next door to us. Our neighbor might be an agnostic, an atheist or a person of another religious faith.

However, that was not at all the case. Neighbors in Jewish Old Testament times were family, all descendants of Jacob. Jacob's twelve sons became twelve large family units. Known as Israelites, they were brothers and sisters, relatives—a close-knit, tribal people. All were members of God's covenant community.

---

[12] "Theologically important is James 2:8 . . ." "It signifies the law as given by the (King)." ". . . It is better to give it the more specific sense and . . . to see in it a reference to God as the (King) who makes law." Gerhard Kittel, *Theological Dictionary of the New Testament* (Grand Rapids: Wm. B. Eardmans, 1965).

[13] See Acts 12:20 as an example of this use of the word.

[14] James 1:25

Therefore, in this Jewish culture, *your neighbor* was family in both the genealogical and religious sense. Because of this, when God commanded them to "love your neighbor as yourself," He was telling them to "love one another"! This becomes clear when looking at the context of these words as found in Leviticus.

> Do not go about spreading slander among *your people*. Do not do anything that endangers *your neighbor's* life. I am the LORD. Do not hate *your brother* in your heart. Rebuke *your neighbor* frankly so you will not share in his guilt. Do not seek revenge or bear a grudge against one of *your people*, but love *your neighbor* as yourself. I am the LORD.[15]

As I looked at this passage more closely, I could hear the rhythmic use of "your people/your neighbor" and "your brother/your neighbor." To these people, a neighbor was a brother—their people. Indeed, they were being commanded to *love one another*.

Because "love your neighbor as yourself" was the closest equivalent that could be found to the yet unwritten "love one another," James uses it to introduce the King's Law. For those who lived according to that law, there was freedom and blessing. He goes on to urge those who were "believers in our glorious Lord Jesus Christ"[16] not to favor the rich or dishonor the poor who were part of their fellowship, because to do so would not be in keeping with the King's Law. Rather, they were to conduct themselves in keeping with "the law that gives freedom."

> Speak and act as those who are going to be judged by *the law that gives freedom*, because judgment without mercy will be shown to anyone who has not been merciful. Mercy triumphs over judgment![17]

---

[15] Leviticus 19:16-18
[16] James 2:1
[17] James 2:12-13

James contrasts "the law that gives freedom" with what he calls the "whole law," meaning the law that was given to Moses and governed the former covenant. James speaks of this law when he writes, "Whoever keeps the *whole law* and yet stumbles at just one point is guilty of breaking all of it."[18] Apparently, in James' experience, the Law of Moses was not *a perfect law that gave freedom!* Rather, in large part, the *whole law* lacked the provision of mercy.

MY PROVIDENTIAL ENCOUNTER WITH THE LAW

As I'm writing this part of the book, my wife and I are guests in a home in the beautiful city of Piedmont, California. We can look out the front window and see the city of San Francisco and the Golden Gate Bridge. Early each morning, I've been driving down the narrow winding streets to the picturesque Montclair Village to gain Internet access and continue my writing.

Parking is at a premium in Montclair Village, and the meter eagerly gobbles up ten quarters for the two-hour maximum. A couple of mornings ago, I fed the parking meter, duly noting the time, and then began writing. I kept an eye on my watch as the metered time was ending.

When the two hours were almost up, I stepped out of the café . . . only to see a police officer next to my car. I was shocked to think that the meter had expired and quickly took about a dozen steps to where he was standing. I arrived to hear the faint whirring sound of the little computerized ticket-writer he held in his hand. It spit out a parking violation—$35.

I wanted to plead for mercy. I had paid the full price for the two hours. It seemed impossible that I could have been more than thirty

---

18 James 2:10

seconds over the allotted time. It was as if the officer had noticed that the meter was so close to expiring that he paused, took a deep breath of morning air and then pushed the button on his little ticket-writer as the word "expired" popped up. It had to have been that close!

There was no point in arguing the facts. I had kept the law for 120 minutes, but at 121 minutes, I was as guilty as if I had parked all two hours without feeding the meter. I meekly took the ticket from his hand and managed a weak, "Thank you."

The rest of the day was not the same. I felt paranoid, braking sharply when I noticed the front edge of my bumper going slightly into the wide white line at a pedestrian crossing. I reflexively jerked the steering wheel to the left when I saw the front wheel of a parked car pointed into my lane—only to realize no one was in the car. A sense of dread hung over me for the rest of that day and into the next. It seemed that I was constantly breaking the law.

I felt no freedom. The law seemed to loom over me. In fact, my focus was no longer on driving safely; it was now on the law and on the paranoia that came from seeing how often I seemed to be breaking it!

I'm not saying that the law is "bad" or "wrong." What I am saying is that the law typically does not *create* freedom. In contrast, James saw that the King's Law was a perfect law, a law that gave freedom.

I think that is what Jesus had in mind when He said, "For my yoke is easy and my burden is light"[19] and "My command is this: Love each other as I have loved you."[20] He has come to set us free

---

[19] Matthew 11:30
[20] John 15:12

from slavery to sin and the law that gave sin authority over us. He tells us, "If the Son sets you free, you will be free indeed."[21]

Paul also saw this freedom as a prime feature of the New Covenant, one he was unwilling to compromise.

> It is for freedom that Christ has set us free. Stand firm, then, and do not let yourselves be burdened again by a yoke of slavery. Mark my words! I, Paul, tell you that if you let yourselves be circumcised, Christ will be of no value to you at all. Again I declare to every man who lets himself be circumcised that he is obligated to obey the *whole law*.[22]

Clearly, living under the *whole law* was not the same as the freedom experienced by those who now embraced the King's Law!

In writing to the new followers of Jesus, James knew that those who had lived under the Law given by Moses had to know *the perfect law, the law that gives freedom, the King's Law!* They were living in a New Covenant with a new law. The King's Law contained the One Command Jesus gave—Love one another as I have loved you.

> If you really keep the royal law found in Scripture, "Love your neighbor as yourself," *you are doing right*.[23]

James' words "you are doing right" reassure us and affirm a very simple code of conduct for believers in the New Covenant. When you love one another, you are doing what God desires of you. It is indeed a very simple code of conduct, but one that fulfills the Law given in the previous covenant.

---

[21] John 8:36
[22] Galatians 5:1-3
[23] James 2:8

In my understanding, this would have been James' early teaching about Jesus' Command to "the twelve tribes scattered among the nations"[24] as well as to the Jerusalem church he pastored. A new law had been introduced, not one that diminished the whole law, but rather one that fulfilled and superseded it. It was the *King's Law*.

James wasn't the only early writer of Scripture to use the word "law" in a new light. Paul introduces us to the *Law of Christ* in the first letter he wrote—to the believers in Galatia.

I'd explore that next.

---

[24] James 1:1

CHAPTER 16

THE LAW OF CHRIST

"The Law of Christ" was a phrase in Scripture I had never really considered. Even though I was a follower of Jesus and had embraced the New Covenant, I seemed to be more familiar with the Law of Moses than I was with the Law of Christ. I knew that the Law of Moses generally referred to the first five books of the Old Testament and contained the Ten Commandments. So whenever I came across the word "law" in reading the New Testament, I had automatically assumed it was a reference to the Law of Moses.

But recognizing Jesus' Commandment had opened up a whole new realm of understanding for me. Now when I read the words of Paul to the Galatians, they took on a new and heightened meaning.

Carry each other's burdens, and in this way you will fulfill *the law of Christ.*[1]

As I considered this phrase, I noticed some interesting parallels between James and Paul as writers of New Testament letters. Neither of them was one of the twelve disciples who learned from Jesus for three years. Yet many believe these two leaders were the earliest writers of New Testament Scriptures. Although Paul would go on to write another dozen New Testament letters, Galatians—the

---

[1] Galatians 6:2

one in which he introduces *the Law of Christ*—was likely his first letter.

As with James, Paul is writing this letter without the benefit of having been present the night Jesus announced the New Covenant and gave the New Commandment. Furthermore, he, like James, is writing this letter some thirty years before John would record Jesus' actual words, "My command is this: Love each other as I have loved you."[2] Therefore, Paul's introduction of the phrase "Law of Christ" is extremely insightful and no doubt came as one of the special revelations he received from God.

The instruction given by Paul in his letter to the Galatians helped me in a number of ways. First, it simply introduced the phrase "Law of Christ." Now for the first time, I recognized that there was another option besides the Law of Moses. There was the Law of Christ.

Even as the Law of Moses contained Ten Commandments, the Law of Christ contained One Commandment. To me that gave new meaning to some of the uses of the word "law" in the New Testament. There were clearly times that the word "law" was referring to the Law of Christ, rather than the Law of Moses.

Second, Paul's introduction to the Law of Christ helped me understand what Jesus' Command looks like in real-life, practical terms. In 1 John 3:16, John the apostle writes, "This is how we know what love is: Jesus Christ laid down his life for us. And we ought to lay down our lives for our brothers."[3] Although I may not be called upon to physically die for my friends, whenever I help one of my brothers or sisters carry their excessively heavy burden, I am obeying Jesus' Command and fulfilling the Law of Christ.

---

[2] John 15:12
[3] 1 John 3:16

Nearly all of us experience a crushing burden at some point in our lives. It's the kind of load that would tip over your wagon if someone did not come along to give you aid in that moment.

No doubt, there is a direct link between the phrase "carry each other's burdens" and the words written immediately before it.

> Brothers, if someone is caught in a sin, you who are spiritual should restore him gently. But watch yourself, or you also may be tempted. *Carry each other's burdens,* and in this way you will fulfill the law of Christ.[4]

The word "burden"[5] used here means an "excessive load" — something we are not designed to carry. It might well refer to a character flaw or some personal weakness in a brother or sister's life that has made them vulnerable to a particular sin. This vulnerability has contributed to their being ensnared by evil. The Law of Christ, with its One Command to love one another, would move us toward this brother or sister in his or her time of difficulty, rather than away from him or her. It would motivate us to restore them. The Command of Jesus Christ would make us gentle in our life-giving effort. It would also compel us to act with humility rather than judgment, recognizing that we are not immune to similar temptations.

When I obey the Command of Christ, I am moved with compassion to put a shoulder under the excessive burden of a brother or sister in need. When I help someone, I fulfill the Law of Christ.

It is clear that Paul's reference to the Law of Christ was more than a passing fancy from his use of it a second time. This time he is writing his first letter to the church at Corinth.

---

[4] Galatians 6:1-2

[5] James Strong, *The New Strong's Exhaustive Concordance of the Bible* (New York: Nelson, 1984).

I . . . am under *Christ's law*.[6]

Paul wrote this in the context of his compelling passion to preach the Good News about Jesus Christ to people wherever he went. He had a strong desire to influence as many as possible to put their faith in the Savior. Again, here it is in his words:

> Though I am free and belong to no man, I make myself a slave to everyone, to win as many as possible. To the Jews I became like a Jew, to win the Jews. To those under the law I became like one under the law (though I myself am not under the law), so as to win those under the law. To those not having the law I became like one not having the law (though I am not free from God's law but am under *Christ's law*), so as to win those not having the law. To the weak I became weak, to win the weak. I have become all things to all men so that by all possible means I might save some.[7]

For me, Paul's train of thought here is a bit difficult to follow, yet it's very significant. Because of my quest to understand the Command of Christ, I was immediately drawn to his reference to *Christ's law*. I was struck by how real the *Law of Christ* was to Paul.

From his life experience before conversion to faith in Jesus, Paul knew what it was to live under the law given to Moses. He describes his past spirituality as "a Hebrew of Hebrews; in regard to the law, a Pharisee . . . [and] as for legalistic righteousness, faultless."[8]

Although he was willing to identify with those now living

---

[6] 1 Corinthians 9:21

[7] 1 Corinthians 9:19-22

[8] Philippians 3:5-6

under the Law of Moses, Paul knew that he no longer lived at that address. However, he was willing to return to that place to win someone who still lived there.

To those under the law I became like one *under the law* (though I myself am not under the law).[9]

In the Greek language, "under the law" is *hupo* (under) *nomos* (law). Paul had lived *hupo nomos* (under the law), but he didn't live there any longer.

In addition, Paul wanted to win people who knew nothing about the Law of Moses. Here's how he says it:

I became like one *not having the law* . . . so as to win those not having the law.[10]

Here, Paul combines two Greek words to mean "not having the law"—*a* (without) and *nomos* (law)—*anomos*. You could think of it somewhat like our use of the words "moral" and "amoral."

But Paul didn't live here either. He was not under the law (*hupo nomos*), and yet he was not without law (*anomos*). Here is how he put it:

I am not free from God's law but am *under Christ's law*.[11]

Paul was very aware that although he was no longer under the Law of Moses, he was still subject to God's Law. He was not a lawless man. He knew there was another alternative—*the Law of Christ!* The Law of Christ was now God's Law for Paul; that was his current address! Living there was so important to Paul that he was willing to go to any length to see people everywhere join him. He wanted to win

---

[9] 1 Corinthians 9:20
[10] 1 Corinthians 9:21
[11] 1 Corinthians 9:21

them to Jesus, the Messiah.

There was one more surprise for me in this passage. From reading most Bible translations of this verse, I was left with the impression that although Paul no longer lived *under* (*hupo*) the Law of Moses, he now lived *under* (*hupo*) the Law of Christ. However, I now discovered from a closer look at the Greek text that that is not what he wrote. Rather, Paul introduced another word to describe where he lived. That word is *ennomos*. Literally, Paul is saying that he now lived *in* the Law of Christ, not *under* it.

Does that make a difference? Apparently, Paul thought it did. Living *under* something implies weight or heaviness. Living *in* something implies abiding, shelter, protection, being at home or at rest. In Strong's Greek concordance, he strengthens this thought when he describes the word *en* as a "position" or "state" and then adds "i.e., a relation of rest."[12] I believe this is what Paul referred to when he says, "live a life of love."[13] It was to be a lifestyle of keeping the Command of Christ—to love one another as He has loved us.

I certainly had something to learn from Paul; I lacked the clarity that he had about his position in relationship to God's Law. As a Pharisee of Pharisees, he had lived much of his life *under* the Law (*hupo nomos*) of Moses, but that was no longer his home. He now lived *in* the Law of Christ (*ennomos Christou*).

According to Paul, the whole Law was fulfilled by obeying Jesus' Command to love one another. He points this out in Galatians—the same letter in which he introduces the Law of Christ.

You, my brothers, were called to be free. But do not use

---

[12] James Strong, *The New Strong's Exhaustive Concordance of the Bible*
[13] Ephesians 5:2

your freedom to indulge the sinful nature; rather, *serve one another in love*. The entire law is summed up in a single command: "Love your neighbor as yourself."[14]

Even as James drew this sentence from the Torah, calling it the King's Law, Paul, too, uses this same scriptural quotation—"Love your neighbor as yourself"—as being the equivalent of "love one another." In saying that "the entire law is summed up in a single command," Paul was agreeing with the One Command Jesus gave. He reiterates this truth in his most systematic teaching—his letter to the Romans.

> Owe nothing to anyone except *to love one another*; for he who loves his neighbor has fulfilled the law. For this, "You shall not commit adultery, you shall not murder, you shall not steal, you shall not covet," and if there is any other commandment, it is summed up in this saying, "You shall love your neighbor as yourself." Love does no wrong to a neighbor; therefore, love is the fulfillment of the law.[15]

To Paul, the Law of Christ was the law of love. Living in the Law of Christ was simply living a life of love. I believe this is what Paul had in mind when he wrote, "Therefore, as we have opportunity, let us do good to all people, especially to those who belong to the family of believers."[16]

In my personal journey of discovering the Law of Christ, I've had to take a new look at words of Scripture that were already very familiar to me. Yet another portion of Scripture I've had to reconsider are the letters of Peter.

What did he have to say about Jesus' Command?

---

[14] Galatians 5:13-14
[15] Romans 13:8-10 NAS
[16] Galatians 6:10

CHAPTER 17

LOVE COVERS, LOVE CONFRONTS

From reading the Gospels, I'd remembered Peter as a crusty, opinionated, outspoken, arrogant, sword-swinging fisherman from the region of Galilee. He was a man's man. It seemed that he never lacked the courage to say what he was thinking and appeared to have a rather high opinion of himself. He certainly didn't seem like the kind of man that went around passing out flowers to people and talking about love all the time.

However, thirty years later Peter has matured into a seasoned apostle who is writing his first letter. In it he says things like, "Now that you have purified yourselves by obeying the truth so that you have sincere love for your brothers, love one another deeply, from the heart. For you have been born again."[1]

From my previous vantage point, I wouldn't have seen these words as tied to Jesus' Command. But now that connection seemed unmistakable.

Peter was at the Passover meal that historic night when Jesus "took bread, gave thanks and broke it, and gave it to them, saying, 'This is my body given for you; do this in remembrance of me.' . . . [Then] after the supper he took the cup, saying, 'This cup is the new covenant in my blood, which is poured out for you.' "[2]

---

[1] 1 Peter 1:22-23
[2] Luke 22:19-20

But Peter seemed a bit distracted when minutes later Jesus said, "A new command I give you: Love one another. As I have loved you, so you must love one another."[3] I say "distracted" because immediately before introducing the New Command, Jesus had told them that He would be leaving soon and they wouldn't be able to go with Him.[4]

Peter was used to going places with Jesus. In fact, he was invited to go places that other disciples weren't. It didn't seem to sit very well with him that he was not being given a special invitation to go with Jesus on this journey. Indeed, Peter's immediate words after Jesus gave the New Command had nothing to do with what Jesus had just said. Instead, he was stuck on Jesus' leaving without him.

Fortunately, Jesus repeated the Command two more times before the evening was over, owning it as "My Command." Apparently, somewhere along the line, Peter got it. Now thirty years later, he writes the Command twice in his first letter:

> Now that you have purified yourselves by obeying the truth so that you have sincere love for your brothers, *love one another* deeply, from the heart.[5]

> Above all, *love each other* deeply, because love covers over a multitude of sins.[6]

What I noticed is that Peter surrounds the Command in these two accounts with words like "above all," "deeply," and "from the heart." When used individually these words are very powerful, but when combined around one thought—love one another—they have

---

[3] John 13:34
[4] See John 13:33-37
[5] 1 Peter 1:22
[6] 1 Peter 4:8

even more expansive implications.

What's unique about how Peter "got it" is the thought that he attaches to loving one another:

. . . because love covers over a multitude of sins.

I think Peter understood the importance of love covering a multitude of sins from his own personal experience. That lesson was gleaned from two of the longest nights Peter had ever lived through.

The first was the night of the Last Supper. After breaking the bread and sharing it with The Twelve, Jesus gave them the cup as He announced the New Covenant. Once the Passover meal was over, He washed His disciples' feet as an example of His love and a model of servant leadership. He then told them that He would be leaving and gave them the New Command.

Then Jesus took the disciples to pray with Him in the Garden of Gethsemane. As Jesus confronted what lay ahead, His agony was palpable; three times He alternated between prayers that sought an easier way and those of surrender to His Father's will. Then came the moment of His betrayal. As they came to arrest Him, Peter took a couple of swings with his sword—netting one ear in the process.[7]

After Jesus' arrest, authorities questioned Him. Peter had chosen to follow at a distance to see the outcome. It was a cold night, and he blended into a mixed crowd of servants, soldiers and the curious who were warming themselves around an open fire in the court-yard. Suddenly, a young servant girl pointed at Peter and spoke.

"You also were with Jesus of Galilee," she said.

---

[7] See John 18:10

But he denied it before them all. "I don't know what you're talking about," he said.

Then he went out to the gateway, where another girl saw him and said to the people there, "This fellow was with Jesus of Nazareth."

He denied it again, with an oath: "I don't know the man!"

After a little while, those standing there went up to Peter and said, "Surely you are one of them, for your accent gives you away."

Then he began to call down curses on himself and he swore to them, "I don't know the man!"

Immediately a rooster crowed.[8]

What made this all the more painful was Peter's bold response just hours earlier. Jesus had said that all of them would abandon Him that night, but Peter argued otherwise. The exchange went as follows:

Peter replied, "Even if all fall away on account of you, I never will."

"I tell you the truth," Jesus answered, "this very night, before the rooster crows, you will disown me three times."

But Peter declared, "Even if I have to die with you, I will never disown you."[9]

But now, after the rooster crowed, what was happening must have been like a nightmare that wouldn't end.

The Lord turned and looked straight at Peter. Then Peter

---

[8] Matthew 26:69-74
[9] Matthew 26:33-35

remembered the word the Lord had spoken to him: "Before the rooster crows today, you will disown me three times." And he went outside and wept bitterly.[10]

I think the agony Peter was experiencing that long night goes way beyond description. He had denied his Lord. The next day Jesus was crucified. This was followed by the disciples spending long hours behind locked doors in the grip of fear, uncertainty and numbing doubt. There were no heroes at that moment in history, simply men struggling with their doubts and fears.

Yes, it must have brought great comfort to the disciples when the resurrected Jesus appeared to them as they were huddled behind locked doors. I'm sure it helped when Jesus, a week later, made a special visit to allay the doubts of Thomas, who had been absent when He first visited the soon-to-be apostles.

But I have a sense that the guilt that engulfed Peter lingered on. I don't think he could forget his shameful behavior, the unbelievable cowardice he had displayed on that night. In my opinion, Peter thought it was over for him—that he had disqualified himself. His future was fishing on the Sea of Galilee.

For that reason, I think it was Jesus' third appearance to the disciples after His resurrection that was most significant for Peter. In fact, I believe it impacted Peter so deeply that he was thinking of it thirty years later when he wrote, "Above all, love each other deeply, because love covers over a multitude of sins."[11]

Here's the story surrounding that third appearance. Peter and some of the other disciples had decided to get out of Jerusalem after the mix of devastating and perplexing experiences that accompa-

---

[10] Luke 22:61-62
[11] 1 Peter 4:8

nied the arrest, crucifixion and resurrection of their promised Messiah. Peter and six other disciples were together in one of the small villages on the shore of the Sea of Galilee when Peter announced that he was going fishing.

Peter was a leader. The six others who were present—including John—decided to go with Peter. It was probably late afternoon when they got into the boat, but a night of hard work on the lake failed to net even one small fish. It seemed that they were ready to throw in the towel as morning neared.

They were still about the length of a football field from the shore and the night sky was just starting to turn its first shades of grey when they heard a voice coming across the water. Here's where it gets interesting.

"Friends, haven't you any fish?"

"No," they answered.

He said, "Throw your net on the right side of the boat and you will find some."

When they did, they were unable to haul the net in because of the large number of fish. Then . . . [John] said to Peter, "It is the Lord!" As soon as Simon Peter heard him say, "It is the Lord," he wrapped his outer garment around him (for he had taken it off) and jumped into the water. The other disciples followed in the boat, towing the net full of fish.[12]

As Peter climbed ashore, he could probably smell breakfast cooking. Fish were frying on the glowing coals. Bread was standing ready. Jesus asked the disciples to bring a few more fish from their

---

[12] John 21:5-8

recent catch to add to the breakfast that He was cooking.

From the moment of that request, it appears that Peter is back in charge. He is on the boat getting the catch to the shore. Apparently it seemed important that they take time to count the fish—153—and examine the quality of the catch as well—large fish. They also noted that the net had not been torn in spite of the astonishing size of the catch. After all, they were fishermen, and these things were important to them.

Then Jesus announced that breakfast was ready and again took the role of a servant as He gave the fish and bread to the seven hungry fishermen. When they had eaten their fill, Jesus turned His attention to only one of the seven fishermen present—Peter. It would now become clear that for all practical purposes this meeting was about him and him alone.

> When they had finished eating, Jesus said to Simon Peter, "Simon son of John, do you truly love me *more than these?*" [13]

The cast is assembled on the shore. The stage is set for this critical moment in Peter's life.

"More than these?" It had been three years since Jesus had first called to Simon Peter, "Come, follow me . . . and I will make you fishers of men," as he was fishing on this very lake.[14] But now Peter has said, "I'm going out to fish."[15] Jesus is calling him from his fishing for the second time.

"More than these?" As Jesus asked this question, He may well have fixed His gaze on the net full of fish. He may have been

---

[13] John 21:15
[14] See Matthew 4:19
[15] John 21:3

reminding Peter of the bold declaration he had made in front of the other disciples only days earlier at the Passover Meal: "I will lay down my life for you."[16] Peter had even insinuated that his allegiance to Jesus was superior to that of the other eleven disciples when he said, "Even if all fall away, I will not."[17]

Now Peter is center stage. Jesus is reminding him of his own words. The question is his to answer: "Simon son of John, do you truly love me more than these?"

"Yes, Lord," he said, "you know that I love you."

Jesus said, "Feed my lambs."

Again Jesus said, "Simon son of John, do you truly love me?"

He answered, "Yes, Lord, you know that I love you."

Jesus said, "Take care of my sheep."

The third time he said to him, "Simon son of John, do you love me?"

Peter was hurt because Jesus asked him the third time, "Do you love me?" He said, "Lord, you know all things; you know that I love you."

Jesus said, "Feed my sheep."[18]

Life has a lot to do with competing loves. If our first love is success, God's call to us will be to personal obedience that comes from a motivation of love for Him.

In Peter's case, love for Jesus would be expressed by feeding the

---

[16] John 13:37
[17] Mark 14:29
[18] John 21:15-17

sheep—loving people, Jesus' sheep. That's really the call for all of us. "If you love me, you will obey what I command."[19] "If you obey my commands, you will remain in my love. . . . My command is this: Love each other as I have loved you."[20]

Peter's second unforgettable night was ending. In the first long night, he had denied Jesus three times as he warmed himself by a fire. In the second long night, Jesus had confronted Peter's waffling and had led him to profess his love for Him three times by the warmth of another fire—a fire kindled by his true friend.

Only weeks later, Peter would stand with the other apostles and preach his first sermon. He would boldly declare, "This is what was spoken by the prophet Joel: 'In the last days, God says, I will pour out my Spirit on all people.' "[21] That day 3,000 people would step out of the crowd and become followers of the risen Lord Jesus—the One who had so recently fixed breakfast on the shore for Peter and his fishermen friends.

Once again, I looked at the words that Peter had written thirty years after he had endured these two unforgettable nights.

Above all, love each other deeply, because love covers over a multitude of sins.[22]

I think Peter really believed that he had been disqualified by his shameful denial of his Master and Teacher. In my mind, he didn't consider himself worthy of being called a disciple of Jesus Christ. What's more, the thought of being an apostle was no longer in Peter's picture of his future. But then Jesus confronted him.

---

[19] John 14:15
[20] John 15:10, 12
[21] Acts 2:16-17
[22] 1 Peter 4:8

What about me? What about you? How many of us would have disqualified ourselves if someone hadn't loved us enough to pursue us in our darkest moments?

Although it is true that love covers, love is not a cover-up. Love covers, but it also confronts. Love that confronts doesn't always look the way I may have pictured it or practiced it. In my mind, confrontation has always been something that went like, "Meet me in my office at 3:15 this afternoon!" Or it acted like knocking on someone's door and announcing, "I'm here on the basis of Matthew 18 to talk to you about your sin."

When confronting sin in ourselves or in others, I am learning from Jesus' example that it is important to remember God's amazing qualities of kindness, tolerance and patience. I should never treat these qualities as insignificant or with contempt.

> Or do you show contempt for the riches of his kindness, tolerance and patience, not realizing that God's kindness leads you toward repentance?[23]

Certainly, Jesus' kindness had gotten to Peter that morning. He would never forget the Command that Jesus had given them and the miracle of that life-changing moment on the shore where again he heard Jesus' words, "Follow me!"[24]

As I reconsidered what James, Paul and Peter had to say about love, I also found myself taking a fresh look at other Scriptures. From what I was seeing, the Bible gave little room for a middle ground between love and hate.

I'd next consider this surprising finding.

---

[23] Romans 2:4
[24] John 21:19

CHAPTER 18

DO I LOVE 'EM OR HATE 'EM?

As I explored the depths of Christ's Command to love, I was also confronted with the reality that in our fallen world, the opposite of love is also present—*hate*. And from what I see in the Bible, there must be a very fine line between *love* and *hate*. For instance, in the Ten Commandments God had said:

> For I, the LORD your God, am a jealous God, punishing the children for the sin of the fathers to the third and fourth generation of those who *hate* me, but showing love to a thousand generations of those who *love* me and keep my commandments.[1]

As I read those words, it seemed that God didn't leave any middle ground of indifference between *love* and *hate*. You either love God, or you hate Him.

This truth seems unchanged in the New Testament. In the Apostle John's first letter, he uses *love* and *hate* in the same way, again giving no middle ground between the two. He writes, "Anyone who claims to be in the light but *hates* his brother is still in the darkness. Whoever *loves* his brother lives in the light, and there

---

[1] Exodus 20:5-6

is nothing in him to make him stumble."[2]

John continues:

> If anyone says, "I love God," yet hates his brother, he is a
> liar. For anyone who does not love his brother, whom he
> has seen, cannot love God, whom he has not seen.[3]

Personally, I really don't like it that way. I would prefer a large
area of mushy middle ground between *love* and *hate*, a place where I
could live most of the time. From this mushy terrain of indifference,
I could proclaim in self-defense, "I may not *love* 'em, but I for sure
don't *hate* 'em!"

My Picture of Love and Hate

Love | mushy middle ground | Hate

However, the words "anyone who does not love his brother"
imply that anything less than love falls across the line into the
category of hate. This understanding is supported by Strong when,
in defining the word "hate," he states that one of the meanings of
hate is "to love less."[4] In other words, hate can be defined as
anything less than love or anything loved less. Where love stops,
hate starts. The large, mushy middle ground that I feel comfortable
with does not seem to exist from God's perspective.

One day when my wife's Pontiac Bonneville was being serviced,
she asked to use my Chevy Metro. My car has a three-cylinder
engine (that produces a whopping fifty-five horsepower), a stick

---

[2] 1 John 2:9-10
[3] 1 John 4:20
[4] James Strong, *The New Strong's Exhaustive Concordance of the Bible*

shift and none of the power accessories that we are accustomed to these days. When Patti returned my car later in the day, her first comment as she walked through the door was, "I hate your car!"

My response to her was, "You didn't have to drive it. You could have walked!"

"Well, I don't really *hate* your car," she countered. "I just like it a lot *less* than I like my Pontiac!"

In the scriptural sense, Patti was correct in her usage of the words "love" and "hate." Because of her like-it-less feeling toward my car, she really did hate it in the biblical sense! She loved her Bonneville and hated my Metro!

If scriptural hate is defined as anything less than love, it must begin with indifference and extend all the way to murder on the extreme end. Everything in this continuum of hate is based on selfishness. It is "me first" all the way to "me only," without anyone else on the planet. Although indifference seems much more benign than murder, it leans toward murder from the start.

This theme of love and hate started very early in the record of Scripture. The importance of this topic is revealed by the questions God asks. The first is a simple question directed to Adam and Eve: "Where are you?"[5]

They were hiding. The thought of a stroll with God through the garden filled them with fear—something they had never experienced before. God had given them one command.

> You are free to eat from any tree in the garden; but you must not eat from the tree of the knowledge of good and evil.[6]

---

[5] Genesis 3:9
[6] Genesis 2:16-17

There were many trees in the garden from which God said they could eat. However, they chose the *one* tree from which He had instructed them *not* to eat! Suddenly, they felt exposed—uncovered and ashamed—for the first time.

The reason God asked them the question—"Where are you?"—is not because He had lost track of the man and woman He had created. Rather, He spoke the question because He wanted Adam and Eve to find themselves! They needed to realize what they had done and where their choice had led them. It was important for them to understand that their trust in God had been broken and that consequently they were now doing their very best to hide from Him. Loving relationship between the Creator and His creation had been interrupted, so God asked the question to get the man and woman to think about that break.

The second question we hear God asking is directed to one of Adam and Eve's sons: "Then the LORD said to Cain, 'Where is your brother Abel?' "[7]

The reason for this question is that the relationship between the two brothers had been broken—badly broken! Actually, Cain had just killed his brother, Abel. Again, God is not asking this question because He doesn't know where to find Abel. He had already heard Abel's blood crying from the ground. Rather, God asks the question to expose Cain's flawed thinking and immoral conduct.

I think these two questions correspond to the two core commandments of the Old and New Covenants. We should all take these two questions to heart. "Where are you?" is God's question to us about the nature of our relationship with Him. "Where is your brother?" is God's question to us about the nature of our relationship with one another.

---

[7] Genesis 4:9a

In the Christian faith, we understand that our relationship with God is restored when we place our faith in His Son, Jesus Christ. Our relationship with one another is restored when we love one another as Jesus commanded us. These are the *two core commandments* of Christian discipleship as taught in the New Testament.

I find the first question Cain asked God to be indicative of the greatest problem we face in our relationship with one another: "Am I my brother's keeper?"[8]

Cain's self-absorbed attitude moved quickly from *indifference* toward his brother to actually *murdering* him. No wonder these words in New Testament Scripture refer back to this incident:

> This is how we know who the children of God are and who the children of the devil are: Anyone who does not do what is right is not a child of God; nor is anyone who does not love his brother.

> This is the message you heard from the beginning: We should *love one another*. Do not be like Cain, who belonged to the evil one and murdered his brother.[9]

It was becoming clear to me that hate was a continuum that started with apathy or indifference and continued all the way to murder.

I gained more insight into this when a group of pastors in our city started meeting to learn how to love one another. Dave, one of my pastor friends, helped me see the other half of the picture. He pointed out that love also is a continuum that starts with concern!

This has become an extremely significant insight for me. If hate is a continuum that starts with indifference and ends with murder,

---

[8] Genesis 4:9b

[9] 1 John 3:10-12

love is a continuum that starts with concern and extends all the way to giving your life so another can live. That understanding allowed me to see why I could find no mushy middle ground between love and hate; there wasn't any! Concern stands right next to indifference, but they lean in opposite directions. Just as indifference leans toward murder, concern leans toward laying down one's life for another.

God's Picture of Love and Hate

Love Continuum   **Hate Continuum**

Dying for another <--- Concern | Indifference ------------> Murder

---

As the pastors in our city continued to meet and build loving relationships, I saw the scriptural basis for the thought my friend Dave had brought to the table. This theme of *concern* is found in the prelude to Paul's well-known teaching about love in 1 Corinthians 13. There Paul introduces the theme by comparing our relationship with one another to the parts of a human body. For one part of the body to say it has no need of the other parts is unimaginable. Paul puts it this way:

> And the eye cannot say to the hand, "I have no need of you"; nor again the head to the feet, "I have no need of you."[10]

And Paul continues:

> God has combined the members of the body and has given greater honor to the parts that lacked it, so that there

---

[10] 1 Corinthians 12:21 NKJV

should be no division in the body, but that its parts *should have equal concern for each other*.[11]

Rather than living as if we don't need each other, Paul says that we "should have equal *concern* for one another." In my understanding, this *concern* is the place where love starts.

To me it was becoming clear that Paul saw this "equal concern" as the secret to being united, the way we keep from being divided from one another. I believe that Christian unity is never achieved when unity itself is the end we seek. Attempts at unity inevitably fail when they are approached in this manner. Rather, unity is found as we love one another. It is a gift God gives us, and we guard it by our obedience to Jesus' Command.

I now see that only His selfless love can motivate us to be concerned for another part of the body and begin this journey of love. Love, starting with genuine concern for one another, will guard against breaking the unity of the Spirit. Love is the antidote for division among believers. The best way for me to guard that precious gift of unity is to obey the Command that Jesus gave. With that in mind, I took another look at what John had written.

> We love because he first loved us. If anyone says, "I love God," yet hates his brother, he is a liar. For anyone who does not love his brother, whom he has seen, *cannot* love God, whom he has not seen. And he has given us this command: Whoever loves God must also love his brother.[12]

I was struck by the fact that I cannot love God if I am indifferent toward my brothers and sisters. I cannot be a lover of God and fail

---

[11] 1 Corinthians 12:24-25
[12] 1 John 4:19-21

to keep Jesus' Command to "love one another."

"BECAUSE IT IS THE LORD'S COMMAND"

As part of my personal journey of discovery, I was reading Adam Clarke's commentary,[13] written in the early 1800s, on John's account of the Gospel. Clarke was commenting on Jesus' words "that ye love one another." As part of this commentary, he gave a brief but very insightful account of a story about the Apostle John as told by Jerome, a fourth-century Christian leader.

For a couple of years, I looked for Jerome's original account of this story. From what Clarke had said, it seemed I would find it in Jerome's commentary on Galatians. When my travels would take me near major seminary libraries, I would ask for help in finding it. Finally my search came to a successful conclusion one Friday afternoon when the head reference librarian at Loyola Marymount University was assisting me. He was looking in the *Patrologia Latina* database via the Internet. Suddenly, I spotted the quote I had been looking for highlighted on the monitor! (That was the good news. The bad news was that it was in Latin. Apparently Jerome's commentary on Galatians had never been translated into English.)

Having found it (and a good translator), I now know a little more about John's story as Jerome told it.

In writing his commentary on Galatians, Jerome came to the following words Paul had written:

Therefore, as we have opportunity, let us do good to all people, especially to those who belong to the family of believers.[14]

---

[13] Adam Clarke, *Commentary on the New Testament*, Vol. 6 (written 1810-1826), (Albany: AGES Digital Library, 1997), 277.

[14] Galatians 6:10

These words brought to mind a story Jerome had heard, carried down through oral tradition, about John. Jerome tells of a time when John, whom he calls "the blessed evangelist," lived in Ephesus.[15] He was very advanced in age and would be carried by his students to gatherings of believers. Inevitably, he would be asked to address the people. It seems that John would not engage in small talk. When asked to speak, he would say one thing: "Children, love one another!"

Growing weary of hearing him say the same thing over and over, the students and brothers that were close to John asked him, "Teacher, when given the opportunity to speak, why do you always say the same thing?"

John gave them the reason in this answer: "Because it is the Lord's command and if only it be done, it is enough!"[16]

Knowing John's heart, as he expressed it in everyday life and as captured for us in Jerome's story, was very meaningful to me. John personally had no room for apathy. Everything was passionate love; he continually brought the command to them. That in itself pushed the hate away; it was enough!

This story only serves to remind us of the significance of the One Command that Jesus gave us—"Love one another as I have loved you."

Yet in all of what I was discovering, a major piece was missing. The words kept coming back to me, "as I have loved you." I was beginning to realize that the basis for loving others was knowing

---

[15] John the apostle was exiled to the Island of Patmos by Roman emperor Domitian. Shortly after the death of Domitian in A.D. 96, John is believed to have returned to Ephesus where he lived until his death.

[16] S. EUSEBII HIERONYMI STRIDONENSIS PRESBYTERI COMMENTARIORUM IN EPISTOLAM AD GALATAS LIBRI TRES, 517-518.

God's love for me. Fortunately for me, that was a lesson I'd begun learning earlier in life.

It was introduced in a most unforgettable way.

CHAPTER 19

THE BRIDGE: WORDS I WANT TO HEAR

After discovering and understanding Jesus' Command, I knew I wanted obedience to His command to become my lifestyle. I had the information, but how would I get to the place where I could really love others as Jesus loves me?

I realized that living a life of love requires that I have a personal reservoir of love from which to draw. Beyond that, the reservoir must have a source—a rainfall, a spring, a stream or a river—that continually replenishes it. It is imperative that I arrive at a place where I know I won't run out of love. Where is that place? How do I get there? Where is the bridge that will take me to that desired destination?

I had been asking those questions for years. It was about sixteen years ago that I learned a life-changing lesson in a very personal way. I learned that you can't give to others what you don't have yourself. Here's how it happened.

After nearly twenty-four years in full-time pastoral ministry, I realized that I needed to take a sabbatical. That was generally unheard of in the circles in which I ran. Usually when pastors got as tired as I felt, they simply resigned from their position and sought another congregation.

I was fortunate to be serving a congregation that loved Patti and me dearly. In addition, I was surrounded by a wonderful group of elders and a staff that were very supportive. They were receptive to the idea of my taking a leave.

As thoughts of a sabbatical took shape, I got a clear sense that Patti and I were to apply for admission to a short-term discipleship-training school. This was a rather improbable place for us to go for several reasons, the first being that I didn't like the sponsoring organization. A number of the most promising young people in my congregation had gone through their program and then vanished into thin air. That didn't sit well with me; I was trying to build my congregation, not give away my best and brightest.

There were other considerations as well. What would our two teenage children do? What about my wife's reluctance to be in a structured program and the large financial cost of the venture? In spite of the sense I had that it was God's plan for us, it seemed unlikely that this was going to happen.

But all the pieces came together, and in a matter of months, we were thousands of miles from our home and enrolled in the program. As it turned out, it would be nearly six months before we returned to our home, family and pastoral duties.

Our first week in the program was nearly disastrous. We were seasoned adults. Being required to submit to a rigid schedule and having little control over our living arrangements, food or assigned work duties was very challenging. To top it off, we didn't have a car, the ultimate means that many of us in the Western world use to escape unpleasant circumstances. This was a huge shock to our sensibilities. It felt like a total loss of control.

Beyond that, we were now part of an eclectic class of sixty students—ages twenty-eight to seventy-three—from thirteen different countries. We were required to attend classes five days a week and to participate in small-group activities.

At the heart of the program was a guest lecturer who spoke to us for two hours each day. We had a different visiting speaker each week. The lectures were held in a large modern classroom. While some of the students scrambled for the front seats, I chose to sit at the very back with Patti.

The first week's speaker was the picture of perfection—way too perfect for someone as tired and flawed as I was. I slid further and further down in my seat as the hours in that first week dragged by.

Week two started with another guest lecturer. To me, it seemed that he was struggling to catch his stride, and I actually felt a bit of sympathy for him in the first hour or so. He had a much more relaxed style, more like a storyteller than a typical lecturer. He spoke to us for two hours on Monday, two more hours on Tuesday and then another two hours on Wednesday.

Wednesday's session ended at lunchtime. As we were walking to the outdoor mezzanine where our meals were served, Patti commented on how much she was enjoying the speaker and asked me what I thought of him. My own emotionless response seemed strange even to me.

"I don't know. I can't remember anything he said."

Patti let it go.

The next day's activities included another two-hour lecture. Once again, I was sitting in the last row. Our speaker was about halfway through his presentation when I suddenly burst out crying—sobbing out loud! No one else in the room was displaying any perceptible emotion in response to the quiet style of teaching and storytelling we were hearing.

To me, it seemed as if time stopped and the attention of every-one in the room was drawn to the strange outburst from the middle-aged man at the back of the large classroom. Crying is never pleasant. Sobbing in a room full of sixty people I hardly even knew was even more distasteful. I fought it from the start, but there was no stopping it.

Immediately Patti's hand was on me—patting my back rapidly as one does in uneasy moments. She whispered assurance to me: "It'll be okay, Honey. It's all right!"

One sentence kept circling through my mind as I struggled to rein in my emotions. "I want to hear my dad say, 'Son, I love you.' " I was fighting these words, trying to keep them from landing and becoming a part of me.

"That's stupid!" I thought. "I've made it this far without hearing those words. Leave it alone!" I tried to squeeze the words out of my mind. I thought of my dad, thousands of miles away and eighty-two years old. "Why trouble him now?" I thought. "He has been a good dad."

Not soon enough, I regained my composure. That night, I started to write my father a letter. It took me three weeks to finish, and by the time I mailed it, I knew that my issue was about something a lot bigger than hearing my dad say, "Son, I love you."

It was about my inability to receive my Heavenly Father's love. It seems that I had constructed a wall around my heart over years of daily living and pastoral ministry. I had built it to keep people from hurting me—to protect myself from careless words, selfish demands and the assorted fickle behavior of humankind. In my thinking, this wall allowed me to filter what I let in and what I kept out. It was my own self-constructed wall of protection.

I was beginning to understand why I couldn't remember anything that our teacher was saying that week. He was telling us stories about the love he as a father had for his children and about God as a Father and of the love He had for His children. In contradiction to his quiet voice and storytelling style, our teacher was swinging a large, well-aimed sledgehammer. And it was hitting a wall that I had built to protect my heart. I couldn't remember anything he said because I was terrified. I knew that if his gentle words kept bashing that wall, it was going to break. And I didn't know what was behind it. What would happen if it came crashing down?

But by now the damage was done, the wall was coming down and the healing had begun. In the three weeks it took me to write the letter, I saw new words in the Bible. I saw that God had told His Son that He loved Him and that He brought Him pleasure. It happened when John baptized Jesus—before He had performed one miracle or taught a single lesson to the crowds.

> Jesus was baptized. . . . And as he was praying, heaven was opened and the Holy Spirit descended on him in bodily form like a dove. And a voice came from heaven: "You are my Son, whom I love; with you I am well pleased."[1]

On another special occasion, God spoke of His love for His Son in the presence of Peter, James and John on the mountain when He was transfigured.

> A bright cloud enveloped them, and a voice from the cloud said, "This is my Son, whom I love; with him I am well pleased. Listen to him!"[2]

---

[1] Luke 3:21-22
[2] Matthew 17:5

"If God told Jesus that He loved Him," I thought, "it must be normal for fathers to tell their sons that they love them!" Maybe my wanting to hear my father's words wasn't stupid after all.

Jesus lived with a sense of His Father's pleasure over Him. He wasn't constantly striving to gain His approval. Jesus' ministry was not done in an attempt to win His Father's love or acceptance. He knew He was loved before He taught the multitudes, healed the sick or fed the hungry. He knew His Father was pleased with Him before He went to the cross to die for the sins of the world.

By the time I had finished the letter to Dad, I understood what I really needed. In the letter I told him that I needed to hear my Heavenly Father speak His love to me. I dropped off the letter at the small post office on campus.

It was weeks later when I heard my name during the afternoon mail call. I stepped forward and took the letter that was being waved over the expectant crowd. A quick glance at the envelope let me know that it was from my dad. His once streamlined writing, learned in his youth, now showed the trembling signs of age. I left the crowd for a place alone.

I opened the envelope. Inside was a full-sized sheet of lined paper. I unfolded it and started to read.

Dear son Gaylord,

Thank you for the letter you wrote to let me know how you feel.

I don't know if I ever said "I love You." I should have said it. I am sorry because I didn't. It would have been better for you.

I love you. I wasn't use to hear this when I grew up.

This is poor letter. Correct mistake. Haven't written letter for years.

Love

Your dad

I read your letter three times. Thank you for it.

I've opened a lot of letters in my life, but this is the best one I've ever received. I can't see any mistakes in it. It's perfect!

Dad's simple words taught me one of the most valuable lessons I have ever learned. You cannot give away what you don't have.

"I love you. I wasn't use to hear this when I grew up."

My dad never heard, "I love you," from his father. And I doubt that his father heard those words from his father either. You cannot give away what you don't have. You cannot give to others something you haven't received yourself.

That was one lesson, but there was another. I was beginning to understand that God was my Father. I had known that truth theologically for many years, but now I was starting to experience what I had only understood intellectually before. God was more than a distant Creator. He was my Father and He loved me deeply. There was no love deficit in Him. He had enough love to go around, enough to fill and overflow every one of us. God *is* love.[3] And He loves me!

Gradually, during our months of sabbatical leave, I learned that I could trust God enough to let Him demolish the wall of protection that I had built around my heart. It was ill-conceived, my own

---

[3] See 1 John 4:16

crude attempt to save myself. The wall I had constructed was actually keeping me from experiencing my Heavenly Father's love; it was keeping His love from nourishing my thirsty soul—a soul that was designed to hear the words, "Son, I love you."

As my trust in Him grew, I accepted the "wall of salvation"[4] that God had provided for my protection. It was the only wall I needed. I was safe. One by one, the voices of self-condemnation were silenced. I could now receive His words of affirmation. I began to have a growing sense of His pleasure over me as one of His children. I began to experience more of my Heavenly Father's love for me.

For the first time, the words of John the apostle had personal meaning to me.

> How great is the love the Father has *lavished* on us, that we should be called children of God! And that is what we are![5]

Like my dad's, "I wasn't use to hear this when I grew up," I wasn't used to thinking of God's love as "lavish." Instead, I'd thought of God's love as being rather carefully measured—as if there was only so much of it to go around. I was more accustomed to thinking thoughts like, "Don't take too much. You don't deserve it anyway. And if you do take some, make sure you don't waste it or you might not get any the next time I'm giving out love!"

Of course, that thinking affected how I loved others. I couldn't help but be constrained in the way I loved those around me. Besides, in my thinking I needed to conserve what love I did have in order to give it to God.

During the time I was learning more about the lavish love of our

---

[4] See Isaiah 60:18
[5] 1 John 3:1

Heavenly Father, Patti and I were in the Philippines for several weeks finishing up the last part of our six-month sabbatical leave. The rather large group of us were guests in a compound that had a very limited water supply. Conservation was imperative. Showers were particularly critical. A small soup can, equipped with a crude wire hook, had been hung on the shower faucet. We were restricted to three soup cans of water per shower. We learned to make do.

However, in the mountain forests outside the city in which we were staying were numerous waterfalls. I'd seen pictures of them. In my mind I imagined the group of us taking a hike.

> As we walk along I begin to hear a low rumble in the distance, almost like a train approaching. It gets louder as we continue up the path. Then I begin to feel vibrations in the ground. Coming around a bend in the path, there it is—a huge waterfall cascading down the mountainside!

> "Let's get in," someone suggests, "and let it shower down over us!"

> "But wait," I cautioned. "Did anyone bring the soup can?"

How ridiculous! But that was the way I had viewed God's love—as doled out in a little soup can.

But now I'm learning of His lavish love—poured out endlessly for me like a waterfall. I've got a completely new paradigm for understanding God's love!

> God has poured out his love into our hearts by the Holy Spirit, whom he has given us.[6]

If I was going to obey the Command Jesus gave—to love one

---

[6] Romans 5:5

another as He loved us—I was going to need an endless supply of love! I needed to be filled with the Holy Spirit continually. Only then could the rivers of His love flow out of me to other thirsty souls.

> Jesus stood and said in a loud voice, "If anyone is thirsty, let him come to me and drink. Whoever believes in me, as the Scripture has said, streams of living water will flow from within him." By this he meant the Spirit, whom those who believed in him were later to receive.[7]

"I Love You"

During our sabbatical, we were separated from our family by thousands of miles for nearly six months. I couldn't help but wonder what it would be like the first time I saw Dad again. Would he say "the words"?

Dad and Mom met us at the airport in San Francisco. It was hello and a handshake from Dad and a big hug from Mom. It was great to see them again, and we enjoyed getting caught up on the latest news during the four-hour drive back to our home in Chico.

Because we live in the same town, I saw Dad a number of times over the weeks that followed. Although I still wanted to hear the words, there was no spoken, "Son, I love you."

Christmas day arrived. We were gathering at Dad and Mom's home to celebrate this special day. Family was trickling in for the meal that would start our time together. As we arrived, I walked into the living room where Dad was in his familiar recliner. As was my habit, I walked toward where he was seated to say hello.

But this time he was on his feet, walking toward me. "I have

---

[7] John 7:37-39

something I want to tell you," Dad said. Our hands met in a welcoming handshake.

"I love you."

"I love you too, Dad!"

It was a moment I will never forget. That was more than fifteen years ago, but I'm crying in Starbucks just writing about it . . . napkins piling up all over! It was such a brave moment for Dad and a long-awaited one for me. He was able to say those words two more times over the months that followed. I'll treasure them forever.

Dad hasn't said them to me for many years now. It would be nice to hear them again, but I really don't crave them. I have always known that he loved me, and that reality will never change.

Besides, I hear them more often now. Although I still have times when fear and doubt try to intrude, I'm getting better at receiving my Heavenly Father's love. I try to start every day with some moments consciously devoted to affirming that life-giving connection. His lavish love is enabling me to grow in personal obedience to Jesus' Command—to love others as He loves me.

When Jesus gave us the New Command, He never intended that we would fulfill it out of sheer willpower, determination or self-discipline. He was counting on us receiving the love of God just as He had received His Father's love. That is why He said,

As the Father has loved me, so have I loved you.[8]

Receiving the Father's love is the bridge that will get us to the place where we were designed to live. His love enables us to "live a

---

[8] John 15:9

life of love." This is what Paul was saying when he wrote, "Be imitators of God . . . as dearly loved children and *live a life of love, just as Christ loved us.*"[9] To live that life of love, we need to fully receive and continually live in the lavish love God has for us as His children.

We can *discover* Jesus' Commandment by intellectually comprehending what He taught. That is a very significant step. However, living a life of love requires more than *discovery;* it requires *recovery* as well. A full *recovery* of Jesus' Command is dependent upon us receiving the Father's love and living in that love.

In the last chapter of this book—as this journey of *discovery* draws to a close—a new journey is only beginning. It is about *recovery*. What if I really lived out the Command of Christ? What if we all did?

That would be a *Love Revolution!*

---

[9] Ephesians 5:1-2

CHAPTER 20

CONCLUSION: TOUCHING THE TITANIC

Today I did something I never dreamed I would do. I touched the Titanic. Actually, it would be more accurate to say that I touched a *piece* of the Titanic—a thick, triangular iron plate with gnarly rivets embedded in it.[1] It was the only artifact in the Titanic Exhibition that the curious were invited to handle. This chunk of metal had been ripped from the ship's hull by impact with an iceberg on the fateful night of April 14, 1912.

By morning's light, more than two-thirds of the 2,224 people who had so recently and hopefully boarded the ship were no longer in the land of the living. The unthinkable had happened. On its maiden voyage, the "unsinkable" Titanic slid out of sight into the frigid waters off Newfoundland.

Seventy-three years later, on September 1, 1985, the Titanic was rediscovered. It was embedded in the ocean floor two-and-a-half miles below the surface of the Atlantic. Since that time, numerous deep-sea explorations have taken amazing pictures of the ship and brought up artifacts for people to view and touch.

As I visited the exhibit, I realized at least two important lessons

---

[1] On April 2, 2007, I went through the Titanic Exhibition at Turtle Bay in Redding, California.

have been learned from this tragic event. First, although a journey can begin well, a lack of vigilance can lead to terrible loss. There is also another lesson we cannot afford to miss. The Titanic was *re-discovered*, but not *recovered!* There is a vast difference between *rediscovery* and *recovery*.

So it is with Jesus' Command.

History reveals that the church started well. A reading of the book of Acts gives evidence that these first believers loved one another deeply. The letters that follow in the New Testament confirm the vibrant growth of faith in Jesus Christ and love for one another among the first Christians.

One of the examples that stood out to me was from A.D. 197. In that year, Tertullian, an apologist and leader in the church in North Africa, gave a real-life description of what living in the Command of Christ looked like. He wrote:

> We have our treasure-chest . . . piety's deposit fund to support and bury poor people, to supply the wants of boys and girls destitute of means and parents, and of old persons confined now to the house; such, too, as have suffered shipwreck; and if there happen to be any in the mines, or banished to the islands, or shut up in the prisons, for nothing but their fidelity to the cause of God's Church, *it is mainly the deeds of love so noble that lead many to put a brand upon us. They say, "See how they love one another!"*[2]

As with the Titanic, one might question whether it was even possible to meet with mishap after such a vibrant start. Nevertheless, Jesus warned His disciples of a time when "many will turn

---

[2] Tertullian, *Tertullian's Apology* (A.D. 197), Chapter 39 (Albany: AGES Digital Library, 1997), 84.

away from the faith and will betray and hate each other"3 and "the love of most will grow cold."4

In His final instructions, Jesus implies that His Command could be lost when He told His followers, "[teach] them to observe—[to guard or protect by never taking your eyes off]5—all things whatsoever I have commanded you."6

I didn't have to look beyond the record of Scripture to see the necessity of guarding this precious Command and the tragic reality of its loss. Consider the young church in Ephesus. Early on, Paul was clearly encouraged by the *faith* and *love* that characterized the believers there. He wrote, "Ever since I heard about your faith in the Lord Jesus and your love for all the saints, I have not stopped giving thanks for you, remembering you in my prayers." 7 It was an excellent start.

But when John wrote to them thirty years later, he mixed his commendation with an impassioned warning:

> You have forsaken your first love. Remember the height from which you have fallen! Repent and do the things you did at first. If you do not repent, I will come to you and remove your lampstand from its place.8

Although the church in Ephesus had many admirable qualities, John recorded their failure to guard Jesus' Command. They did not love one another as they had at first. Their mark of authenticity had been lost. It was imperative that they repent. As a follow-up to this

---

3 Matthew 24:10

4 Matthew 24:12

5 From my earlier comment on Matthew 28:20—see Chapter 4

6 Matthew 28:20 KJV

7 Ephesians 1:15-16

8 Revelation 2:4-5

warning, it is believed that John spent the last years of his long life in Ephesus reminding them often of the Lord's Command.

I know that for me personally, Jesus' Command was lost! When I first saw the Command on May 1, 2002, I assumed that I was the only one who had missed this amazing declaration. However, I soon learned that was not the case; I found no reference to it among the early church fathers. In the five years that followed, I spent thousands of hours in search of the answer to the question, "Whatever happened to Jesus' Command?"

In my search, I came across some hopeful moments of *discovery* in church history. But I have yet to find a point of *recovery*—a time when His Command was broadly given its rightful place in Christian theology and practice.

This is not to say that there have been no pockets of awareness and practice of the Command throughout our long history. Neither am I saying that pockets of obedience do not exist today. On the contrary, I am certain that there have always been and continue to be at this time, groups who live out Jesus' Command.

This loss did not mean that the words Jesus spoke in giving His Command have been lost from Scripture. They have always been in my Bible, even though I did not see them clearly. Rather, the loss has come because something like a fog settled over the Commandment specifically as Jesus gave it. It is as if a cloud obscured the centrality of His Command within Christian thought and practice.

My personal experience has reminded me that it's possible for something to be right in front of us and yet not see it. I preached the longest sermon series in my pastoral ministry more than twenty-five years ago. The series lasted one year; its topic was love. Yet I didn't clearly see the Command Jesus gave us.

I should have been aware of this loss much earlier in my life.

Nearly three decades ago, I was stepping into my first senior pastorate. I had served that congregation as a youth pastor and associate pastor. It had grown significantly during that decade, and now, with the retirement of the founding pastor, I was being asked to assume the lead role.

This change in leadership required the governing body of the congregation to examine the constitution and bylaws that guided this transition. These legal documents contained our statement of purpose, core beliefs and polity—the rules by which we were governed. What had been adequate for a small congregation seemed inadequate for a larger one. It was unanimously agreed that they needed to be updated.

A search was initiated. In addition to our own denominational affiliation, we contacted more than a dozen leading congregations from various Christian persuasions, asking each of them for a copy of their constitution and bylaws.

Having received these, we set aside a room to process the dozen or so examples. We made copies of each and then cut them into pieces and compiled them in stacks based on common themes. These included statements of faith, purpose, polity and organization, to name a few.

Even now, I have a clear picture in my mind of a very significant moment during that project. I am standing in the middle of the room holding the stack of statements of faith—the core beliefs of each church. I distinctly remember turning to look at another leader in the room and asking, "Does it seem strange to you that none of these mentions *loving one another?*"

That was almost 30 years ago. I now know that a majority of Christian denominations make no direct reference to the One Command Jesus gave us—love one another as I have loved you[9]—in their statement of faith and practice.

The informal surveys I've done over the past several years also confirm this lack of understanding. I find an amazingly consistent response when asking the question, "What is Jesus' Command?" Only one in ten people who embrace the Christian faith include "to love one another" in their answer.

Obviously, my surveys do not qualify as scientific. However, they are an indicator of a historical reality that continues to the present. The Command Jesus gave us was lost and is still waiting to be *discovered* by our generation.

PUTTING IT IN PERSPECTIVE

As I think back over this journey of discovery, I am reminded of several key points. First, the subject of this book is very narrow, yet very important—*rediscovering* the lost Command of Jesus. I am not addressing broad areas of theology or church history. Without apology, my focus is the One Command Jesus gave us.

Second, we should never turn this information into criticism of historical figures, the church or Christianity in general. Rather, I urge each of us to *own* church history. It is "our history." Its strengths and victories are ours. So also are its weaknesses and shortcomings. Our response should be one of sorrow for our historic failure to guard Jesus' Command. This will bring us to humble ourselves, to pray and turn from both our personal and historic failure to love one another as Jesus loved us. This repentance will make way for forgiveness, reconciliation and healing of the deep wounds created by our neglect of the Command.

---

[9] John 13:34

Third, hindsight is always 20/20! Our fathers in the faith faced challenges and circumstances that we have never confronted. It is impossible for us to fully understand the difficulties that they had to overcome in their day. Any progress we make in rediscovering Jesus' Command must be carried in humility.

Fourth, we must live in the present. We are making church history in this very moment. Our criticism of the past will change nothing. Yet if we fail to learn from history, we will repeat the mistakes of our past. Our constructive response in discovering, recovering and guarding Jesus' Command will be shown in the history that is being written through our lives today.

Finally, remember it is not about choosing between faith in Jesus Christ or love for one another. It is living with both of them together! It is the New Covenant *and* the New Commandment—inextricably linked in faith and practice.

DISCOVERY

Discovery is, first of all, personal. It happens one individual at a time. I have shared some of my personal journey of discovery with you in the hope that you will start that joyful journey as well. I want you to live the rest of your life as a believer who deeply trusts in Jesus and guards—protects by never taking your eyes off—the Command He gave us.

There is another way you play a strategic role in discovery. You have a sphere of influence. I'm asking you to pass this message on to those you encounter in life so that they too can personally discover Jesus' Command. As you share the Good News about *faith in Jesus Christ* and His Command to *love one another*, the *discovery* of Jesus' Command can spread to family, friends and associates.

There is another facet to *discovery*. The church must *rediscover* the

Command it held in the beginning. The process of *discovery* for a local church may begin with a pastor, congregational leader or small group. Then it can spread to an entire congregation. New believer and membership classes can include training that deliberately includes teaching Jesus' Command.

All branches of the Christian church can place Jesus' Command prominently in their catechisms and statements of faith and practice. Missionary organizations and discipleship movements can *discover* the Command and incorporate it into their training models. Christian theologies must include Jesus' Command in their belief systems. For *rediscovery* to occur, seminaries and schools of biblical studies will need to feature the Command in their course of study.

Discovering Jesus' Command enables us to examine its original splendor. We can begin to imagine what things would have been like if His Command had been the center of Christianity for all these years. We can think through the tragic effects of its loss in both church and world history. We can postulate about what contributed to the catastrophic loss. However, none of that is *recovering* the Command.

RECOVERY

In my thinking, *discovery* is significant—very significant—but *discovery* is not *recovery*.

We must go beyond both personal and church *discovery*. Jesus' Command must not simply become a museum piece for curious fingers to touch. Rather, it must be fully restored to its place as a *core commandment* of authentic Christian faith and practice. That is when *discovery* becomes *recovery*.

When this happens, we can all embrace once again the commands that were held so centrally in the beginning. Those who embrace the two core commands of Christianity will be a living testament.

And this is his [God's] command: to believe in the name of his Son, Jesus Christ, and to love one another as he [Jesus] commanded us.[10]

As we seek to follow both of these commands, I invite you to pray this simple prayer with me.

FILL ME WITH YOUR LOVE

God, thank You for Your awesome creative power and amazing love for me. Thank You for demonstrating Your love through Your Son, Jesus Christ.

Jesus, I believe in You—all that You said, did and are. I believe that You died for my sins and that You were raised from death on the third day.

I am turning from my ways to Your way. With gratitude I receive Your gifts of forgiveness and eternal life. You are my Savior, and I want to guard the One Command You gave—to love one another.

Thank You for showing me the Father, His kindness, compassion and forgiveness. You said, "No one comes to the Father except through Me." I want to learn all You have to teach me about the Father.

God, thank You for being my Father and for Your lavish love for me. I want to be filled with Your love, poured into me by the Holy Spirit. Fill me so full that it becomes a stream—a river— that overflows and refreshes me and everyone I encounter. Empowered by Your Holy Spirit, teach me how to be a true

---

[10] 1 John 3:23

disciple and live a life of love.[11]

Thank you for joining this *Love Revolution* that takes us full circle back to the feet of Jesus—"the author and finisher of our faith."[12] Thank you for hearing His One Command—*Love one another as I have loved you.*

---

[11] If you have just now started your journey as a follower of Jesus, I have given several suggestions in Appendix D about how to grow as a follower of Jesus. You may also email me at *gaylord@gaylordenns.com*

[12] Hebrews 12:2 KJV

An Invitation from the Author

I am encouraging a *Love Revolution*—a growing movement of believers who are committed to (1) faith in Jesus Christ and (2) love for one another. With this in mind, I am urging Christians everywhere to pray for the coming of God's Kingdom, agreeing that His will be done on earth as it is in heaven. I am certain this includes the full *recovery* of Jesus' Command.

If it is the Lord's will, I plan to continue writing on this theme with a focus on *recovering* Jesus' Command. I am interested in receiving short accounts of your personal experience in *discovering* and *recovering* Jesus' Command and living a life of love.

I am also interested in hearing what steps your congregation, denomination or educational institution might be taking to *recover* Jesus' Command.

Please send them to:

    E-mail:
        gaylord@gaylordenns.com

    Surface mail:
        My Story
        P.O. Box 6790
        Chico, CA 95927-6790

I look forward to learning together.

        Love and blessings,

Gaylord Enns

CHAPTER DISCUSSION QUESTIONS

CHAPTER 1: DAYS GONE AWRY

"And we know that in all things God works for the good of those who love him, who have been called according to his purpose."
—Romans 8:28

1. Have you experienced a life-altering crisis? (If you have not, what about someone close to you?)

2. How did it impact your life?

3. In what ways have you seen God at work to bring good out of the difficulty?

4. How can you apply Romans 8:28 to your life?

CHAPTER 2: AN EMPTY TABLE

"Therefore go and make disciples of all nations, baptizing them in the name of the Father and of the Son and of the Holy Spirit, and teaching them to obey everything I have commanded you."
—Matthew 28:19-20

1. What events surround the occasion on which Jesus speaks these words?

2. What proclamation does Jesus give before commissioning them to "make disciples"?

3. What does the author identify as Jesus' embedded definition of disciple making?

4. How can you apply this in your life?

CHAPTER 3: ALL THAT I COMMANDED

"A new command I give you: Love one another. As I have loved you, so you must love one another. By this all men will know that you are my disciples, if you love one another."   —John 13:34-35

1. On what occasion does Jesus introduce this New Command?

2. Prior to reading this chapter, when asked the question, "What is Jesus' Command?" what would your answer have been?

3. Why would we call this Jesus' Command?

4. How can you apply this in your life?

CHAPTER 4: THE EARLY CHURCH FATHERS

". . . and teaching them to obey everything I have commanded you."
          —Matthew 28:20

1. Whom does the author identify as the "early church fathers"?

2. What is the fuller meaning of the word "obey"?

3. What are we instructed to guard?

4. How can you apply this in your life?

Chapter 5: Two Core Commandments

"And this is his command: to believe in the name of his Son, Jesus Christ, and to love one another as he commanded us."

—1 John 3:23

1. When we read "And this is his command," to whom does the "his" refer?

2. When we read "as he commanded us," to whom does the "he" refer?

3. Why does the author call these the "core commandments of Christianity"?

4. How can you apply this in your life?

Chapter 6: You Can Ask a Question

"The King will reply, 'I tell you the truth, whatever you did for one of the least of these brothers of mine, you did for me.' "

—Matthew 25:40

1. What question was troubling the author? Can you identify with his question?

2. Where is "God's new home," and why is this important?

3. Who is the "King" in the above Scripture?

4. How can you apply this in your life?

CHAPTER 7: A BREAKFAST SURPRISE

"If anyone says, 'I love God,' yet hates his brother, he is a liar. For anyone who does not love his brother, whom he has seen, cannot love God, whom he has not seen." —1 John 4:20

1. Why is it impossible to love God if we do not love our Christian brothers and sisters?

2. How is it that when we love one another, we give God a "double hug"?

3. Does Jesus ever come to your house?

4. How can you apply this in your life?

CHAPTER 8: COMPARING THE OLD AND NEW

"This is love: not that we loved God, but that he loved us and sent his Son as an atoning sacrifice for our sins. Dear friends, since God so loved us, we also ought to love one another." —1 John 4:10-11

1. What does the author identify as the core commandments of the Old Testament?

2. What does the author identify as the core commandments of the New Testament?

3. What are some of the significant differences between the two?

4. How can you apply this in your life?

CHAPTER 9: THE TIME IS COMING

" 'The time is coming,' declares the LORD, 'when I will make a new covenant with the house of Israel and with the house of Judah.' "
—Jeremiah 31:31

1. Discuss the when, where and who of both the Old Covenant existing in Jeremiah's time and the promised New Covenant.

2. Why was a new covenant needed?

3. How did God prepare them for this change?

4. How can you apply this in your life?

CHAPTER 10: *NOT* LIKE THE COVENANT

" 'It will not be like the covenant I made with their forefathers when I took them by the hand to lead them out of Egypt, because they broke my covenant, . . .' declares the LORD."   —Jeremiah 31:32

1. Why were the words "not be like" important to the people to whom Jeremiah was speaking?

2. Why are those words important to us today?

3. What change stands out to you as being most significant?

4. How can you apply this in your life?

CHAPTER 11: LISTEN TO HIM!

"A bright cloud enveloped them, and a voice from the cloud said, 'This is my Son, whom I love; with him I am well pleased. Listen to him!' "
—Matthew 17:5

1. What can we learn from the words God spoke to Peter, James and John on the Mount of Transfiguration?

2. What significance do you see in the appearance of Moses and Elijah along with Jesus?

3. Why does the author suggest that Jesus' words have special significance to us today?

4. How can you apply this in your life?

CHAPTER 12: NEW COVENANT, NEW COMMANDMENT

"And he [Jesus] took bread, gave thanks and broke it, and gave it to them, saying, 'This is my body given for you; do this in remembrance of me.' In the same way, after the supper he took the cup, saying, 'This cup is the new covenant in my blood, which is poured out for you.' " —Luke 22:19-20

1. Why are the words "New Covenant" so significant to us?

2. What kind of leadership would you say Jesus modeled?

3. What is the significance of announcing the New Covenant and the New Commandment on the same night?

4. How can you apply this in your life?

CHAPTER 13: ONE NEW PERSON

"His purpose was to create in himself one new man out of the two, thus making peace, and in this one body to reconcile both of them to God through the cross."   —Ephesians 2:15-16

1. Is the New Covenant meant only for Gentiles? Only for Jews? Or for both Jews and Gentiles? Why?

2. What pictures are used in Scripture to demonstrate that the division between Jews and Gentiles would be abolished?

3. How important is the New Command to unity between Christians and between Christian churches?

4. How can you apply this in your life?

CHAPTER 14: LOST AND FOUND?

"Dear friends, let us love one another, for love comes from God. Everyone who loves has been born of God and knows God. Whoever does not love does not know God, because God is love."

—1 John 4:7-8

1. What was Augustine's position about the importance of Jesus' two-part answer to the question about the Law of Moses?

2. What core commandment did Luther emphasize in his teaching, and how did that impact the Christian faith?

3. Why does the author believe Jesus' Command is important to understanding the New Testament letters?

4. How can you apply this in your life?

CHAPTER 15: THE KING'S LAW

"But the man who looks intently into the perfect law that gives freedom, and continues to do this, not forgetting what he has heard, but doing it—he will be blessed in what he does."   —James 1:25

1. What is unique about James and the position he filled?

2. According to the author, why was "love your neighbor as yourself" used by James to define the King's Law?

3. How is it that "the perfect law" gives "freedom"?

4. How can you apply this in your life?

CHAPTER 16: THE LAW OF CHRIST

"Carry each other's burdens, and in this way you will fulfill the law of Christ." —Galatians 6:2

1. What connection do you see between the Law of Christ and Jesus' Command?

2. What do you see as the difference between living *under* the Law of Moses and living *in* the Law of Christ?

3. How could the entire Law be summed up in a single command?

4. How can you apply this in your life?

CHAPTER 17: LOVE COVERS, LOVE CONFRONTS

"Above all, love each other deeply, because love covers over a multitude of sins." —1 Peter 4:8

1. Why were Peter's words, "love covers over . . ." especially meaningful to him?

2. What is the difference between a love that covers and a cover-up?

3. What does Jesus' interaction with Peter teach us?

4. How can you apply this in your life?

Chapter 18: Do I Love 'em or Hate 'em?

"Anyone who claims to be in the light but hates his brother is still in the darkness. Whoever loves his brother lives in the light, and there is nothing in him to make him stumble."   —1 John 2:9-10

1. Why does the Bible give no "mushy middle ground" between love and hate?

2. What does indifference look like? What does concern look like?

3. What relationship do you see between Jesus' Command and unity among Christians?

4. How can you apply this in your life?

Chapter 19: The Bridge: Words I Want to Hear

"How great is the love the Father has lavished on us, that we should be called children of God! And that is what we are!"   —1 John 3:1

1. What kept the author from experiencing God's love?

2. What connection is there between receiving the Father's love and loving one another as Jesus commanded?

3. In what ways do we receive and experience God's love?

4. How can you apply this in your life?

CHAPTER 20: CONCLUSION: TOUCHING THE TITANIC

*"Yet I hold this against you: You have forsaken your first love.
Remember the height from which you have fallen! Repent . . ."*
—Revelation 2:4-5

1. Can you relate to the author's personal discovery of Jesus' Command?

2. In your experience, is there a need among Christians in general to discover Jesus' Command? Explain.

3. How do you understand the author's use of the words "discover" and "recover"?

4. What would your life look like if you became part of a *Love Revolution?*

APPENDICES

APPENDIX A

COMMANDS VS. COMMAND IN THE NEW TESTAMENT

I had a question about Jesus' interchangeable use of the words "commands" (plural) and "command" (singular). Is Jesus talking about one command or many commands? (see John 14:15, 21; 15:10, 12). John also uses the alternating plural and singular in writing his letters (see 1 John 2:3-8; 3:22-24; 5:2-3; 2 John 1:6).

Kittel's *Theological Dictionary of the New Testament* provides the best answer I have come across to explain the mixed use of the plural and singular in these cases:

> The plural "commands" . . . is simply a development of John's favourite concept of unity. . . . The [use of the plural] "commands" always summed up in the one command of love, do not imply a Jewish multiplicity of ordinances, but the radiating of the one "command" out into the manifoldness of the obedient life. . . . It is [the] . . . fulfillment of the commandments as the one command-ment grounded in Jesus.[1]

---

[1] Gerhard Kittel, *Theological Dictionary of the New Testament* (Grand Rapids: Wm. B. Eerdmans, 1965), 554.

APPENDIX B

USES OF "COMMAND" (*ENTELLOMAI* OR *ENTOLE*)
IN THE GOSPELS

The word "command" (*entellomai* or *entole*) is found in all four of the Gospel accounts. It is important to recognize that this word differs from the more frequent use of the *aorist imperative* in the Greek language, which also indicates an authoritative thrust in what is spoken.

THE GOSPEL ACCORDING TO MATTHEW: Matthew uses the word "command" (*entellomai* or *entole*) twelve times. Of the twelve, Jesus applied it universally as His Command in one instance.

> Matthew 28:20: ". . . teaching them to obey everything I have commanded you."

THE GOSPEL ACCORDING TO MARK: Of the ten times the word "command" (*entellomai* or *entole*) is used by Mark, there are none in which Jesus used it to refer to His Command.

THE GOSPEL ACCORDING TO LUKE: The word "command" (*entellomai* or *entole*) is used by Luke five times, but in none of these instances is it applied as His Command.

THE GOSPEL ACCORDING TO JOHN: John uses the word "command" (*entellomai* or *entole*) on fourteen occasions in his account of the Gospel. Of the fourteen times, Jesus applied it universally as His Command in seven unique instances.

> John 13:34: "A new *command* I give you: Love one another. As I have loved you, so you must love one another."

John 14:15: "If you love me, you will obey what I *command*."

John 14:21: "Whoever has my *commands* and obeys them, he is the one who loves me. He who loves me will be loved by my Father, and I too will love him and show myself to him."

John 15:10: "If you obey my *commands,* you will remain in my love, just as I have obeyed my Father's *commands* and remain in his love."

John 15:12: "My *command* is this: Love each other as I have loved you."

John 15:14: "You are my friends if you do what I *command*."

John 15:17: "This is my *command:* Love each other."

APPENDIX C

JESUS' COMMAND IN THE WRITINGS
OF THE EARLY CHURCH FATHERS (A.D. 125-325)

In the years that followed my original search in Bercot's work, I did my own search of the writings of the ante-Nicene fathers and found six direct references to Jesus' Command. One was in the writings of Clement of Alexandria from the end of the second century. Four were in the writings of Cyprian, Bishop of Carthage, from about the middle of the third century. Finally, I found one direct reference in *Apostolic Teaching and Constitution,* a compiled document that was in existence at the end of the third century.

In addition, there are numerous references to *loving one another* without direct reference to the Command given to us by Jesus as the "New Command" or "My Command."

APPENDIX D

GROWING AS A FOLLOWER OF JESUS

I would highlight three areas for you as you start this new life.

1. READING THE NEW TESTAMENT SCRIPTURES

Based on my own personal experience, I would encourage you to start by reading John's Gospel. I recommend reading through it as you would read a letter you have just opened from a friend. (This may take a few days.) Then start over at the beginning and read for more detail, focusing on points you missed the first time. I recommend highlighting some parts of the text that stand out as significant for you. Finally, read it a third time. Look for more details as you go through. Select several verses that seem especially significant for you and memorize them. (Also, memorize the number of the chapter and verse so you can find them easily.)

Following John, I would suggest reading Acts. This is the book that follows John's Gospel. Acts will give you a picture of what life as a follower of Jesus looked like in the beginning. It will also give you a feel for the sequence of events in the first thirty years of Christianity.

I would then suggest looking at John's letters near the end of the New Testament. There are three of them, and they are very short. (Again, I recommend following the "three-step reading approach" I suggest above.)

Following that, I recommend reading Paul's letter to the Ephesians, then Peter's two letters, followed by the letter written by James. Start to intersperse the Gospels according to Mark, Matthew and Luke.

I would suggest that you spend the first year reading in the New Testament. My reasoning is simple: It is the New Covenant—the one that relates directly to you and provides a clear and relevant foundation for your understanding of the Christian faith.

2. PRAYER

Prayer is simply communication with God. It is both talking to Him and listening. The prayer Jesus taught us to pray is a wonderful example. You will find it in Matthew 6:9-13.

You will see many examples of prayer as you read the New Testament. Use these prayers as models as you come across them.

Finally, follow your heart in prayer. Express your honest thoughts and feelings to God. As you would with a loving, earthly father, ask your Heavenly Father for wisdom on decisions in life and for His help in daily living.

3. BEING TOGETHER WITH OTHER FOLLOWERS OF JESUS

It is normal for family to be together. You will notice how this happened as you read Acts. Early Christians got together in big gatherings and in small groups. I would recommend that you adopt this as a pattern for your life.

In our Western culture, gatherings of Christians usually happen in a church building. Some of the buildings are very large, and others are quite small. Some look like a church building and others don't. As part of your prayers to God, ask Him to guide you to a church family who will encourage you in your life of faith in Jesus Christ and remind you to guard Jesus' Command to love one another as He loves you.

APPENDIX E

BIBLE TRANSLATIONS

(KJV) King James Version. Public Domain

(NAS) *New American Standard Bible.* Anaheim: Foundation Press, 1973

(NKJV) *New King James Version.* Nashville: Thomas Nelson, 1982

(NLT) *New Living Translation.* Wheaton: Tyndale, 1996, 2004

(YLT) *Young's Literal Translation of the Old and New Testaments.* Robert Young, 1898

Aramaic New Testament. Khabouris Codex.

Cover: Our thanks to Dr. Michael Ryce for permission to use an image of page 237 of his Khabouris website at http://whyagain.com/KhaburisKhaboris/. This page contains an image of the ancient Aramaic text we know as John 13:34-35. The text shown was written around A.D. 1050. It is believed to have been copied from Aramaic Scripture written as early as the second century.

Bibliography

Augustine. *Enchiridion: On Faith, Hope and Love.* Translated and edited by Albert C. Outler. Albany: AGES Digital Library, 1967.

Bercot, David W., ed. *A Dictionary of Early Christian Beliefs.* Peabody: Hendrickson, 1998.

Brown, Colin, ed. *Dictionary of New Testament Theology.* Grand Rapids: Zondervan, 1986.

Calvin, John. *Institutes of the Christian Religion.* Edited by John T. McNeill. Philadelphia: Westminster, 1967.

——. *The Works of John Calvin* (Calvin's Bible Commentaries, Calvin's Institutes, General Writings, Sermons). Albany: AGES Digital Library, 2000.

Chapman, Gary D. *The Five Love Languages.* Chicago: Northfield, 1992.

Clarke, Adam. *Clarke's Commentary,* 8 vols. Albany: AGES Digital Library, 1997.

d'Aubigne, J. H. Merle. *History of the Reformation in the Time of Calvin,* 4 vols. Albany: AGES Digital Library, 1998.

Denck, Hans. *Selected Writings of Hans Denck.* Edited by E. J. Furcha. Lewiston: Edwin Mellen Press, 1989.

Encyclopedia Britannica. Chicago: Encyclopedia Britannica, Inc., 2001.

Friedmann, Robert. *The Theology of Anabaptism.* Scottdale: Herald Press, 1972.

González, Justo L. *The Story of Christianity.* New York: Harper Collins, 1984.

Grebel, Konrad. *The Sources of Swiss Anabaptism.* Edited by Leland Harder. In *Classics of the Radical Reformation.* Edited by Cornelius J. Dyck. Scottdale: Herald Press, 1985.

Hubmaier, Balthasar. *Classics of the Radical Reformation.* Edited by Wayne Pipkin and John H. Yoder. Scottdale: Herald Press, 1989.

Joris, David. *The Anabaptist Writings of David Joris.* Translated and edited by Gary K. Waite. Waterloo: Herald Press, 1994.

Kittel, Gerhard. *Theological Dictionary of the New Testament.* Grand Rapids: Wm. B. Eerdmans, 1965.

Krahn, Cornelius, ed. *The Mennonite Encyclopedia.* Scottdale: Mennonite Publishing House, 1957.

Luther, Martin. *Good Works, Preface to Romans, Table Talk, 95 Theses, The Large Catechism, The Small Catechism, The Smalcald Articles.* Albany: AGES Digital Library, 2000.

——. *The Martin Luther Collection, 95 Theses, A Commentary on St. Paul's Epistle to the Galatians, Luther's Commentary on the Sermon on the Mount, The Letters of Martin Luther, Watchwords for the Warfare of Life, Prophecies of Luther,* Sermons of Luther (8 vols.), *Works of Luther* (6 vols.). Albany: AGES Digital Library, 1998.

Marpeck, Pilgram. *The Writings of Pilgram Marpeck.* In *Classics of the Radical Reformation.* Translated and edited by William Klassen and Walter Klaassen. Kitchener, Ontario: Herald Press, 1978.

Melanchthon, Philipp. *The Augsburg Confession.* Albany: AGES Digital Library, 1997.

Merriam Webster's Collegiate Dictionary, Tenth Edition. Chicago: Merriam-Webster, Inc., 2000.

Random House Webster's Unabridged Dictionary. Content Copyright 1999, 1997, 1996, 1994, 1993, 1987. Software Copyright 1997, 1996, 1994, 1993 by Lernaut & Haupie.

Roberts, A., and J. Donaldson, eds. *The Ante-Nicene Fathers,* 10 vols. Albany: AGES Digital Library, 1997.

Schaff, Philip, ed. *The Nicene and Post-Nicene Fathers, Series 1,* 14 vols. Albany: AGES Digital Library, 1997.

——. *The Nicene and Post-Nicene Fathers, Series 2,* 14 vols. Albany: AGES Digital Library, 1997.

——. *The History of the Christian Church.* Albany: AGES Digital Library, 1997.

Simons, Menno. *The Complete Writings of Menno Simons.* Translated by Leonard Verduin. Edited by J. C. Wenger. Scottdale: Herald Press, 1956.

Strong, James. *The New Strong's Exhaustive Concordance of the Bible.* New York: Nelson, 1984.

The Ultimate Christian Library. Rio: AGES Digital Library, 2000.

Thompson, Bruce. *Walls of My Heart.* Euclid: Crown, 1989.

Tertullian. *Tertullian's Apology.* Albany: AGES Digital Library, 1997.

Wesley, John. *Notes on the Whole Bible.* Albany: AGES Digital Library, 1997.

———. *The Works of John Wesley, Third Edition Complete and Unabridged.* London, 1872.

———. *The Works of John Wesley,* 14 vols. Peabody: Hendrickson, 1984.

Young, Robert. *Analytical Concordance to the Bible.* Grand Rapids: Wm. B. Eerdmans, 1971.

CONTACT INFORMATION

For Speaking Requests

gaylord@gaylordenns.com

530-891-5599

Gaylord Enns
Servant Leadership Network
P.O. Box 6790
Chico, CA 95927-6790

For more information about
this and other life-changing books,
go online at
www.LoveRevolutionPress.com

Other books published by LRP include:

Uncovering Love, Discovering Soul
By Mary and friends

The Green Ladder
By Steve Shaw

For special pricing on
bulk quantities of this book,
email LRP at
info@LoveRevolutionPress.com
or call
1-530-891-5599